I0025233

The Self, and Other Stories

Creative Interventions in Global Politics

Series Editors: Shine Choi, Cristina Masters, Swati Parashar, and Marysia Zalewski

The landscape of contemporary global politics is complex and oftentimes violent. Yet the urgency to provide solutions or immediate practical actions to this violence oftentimes leads to inadequate knowledge. This is despite the abundance of theoretical, conceptual and methodological tools available – much of this produced through conventional academic disciplines, notably International Relations, Political Theory and Philosophy. But the constraints imposed on these traditional disciplines profoundly limit their ability to incorporate and make effective use of more creative and innovative methodologies found in other disciplines and genres.

This series provides a unique opportunity to offer creative intellectual space to work with an eclectic and rich range of disciplines and approaches including performative methodologies, storytelling, narrative and auto-ethnography, embodied research methodologies, participant research, visual and film methodologies and arts-based methodologies.

Titles in the Series

Sites of Dissent: Nomad Science and Contentious Spatial Practice
   Alissa Starodub
Pedagogy as Encounter: Beyond the Teaching Imperative
   Naeem Inayatullah
The Lived International: A Life in International Relations
   Stephen Chan
Tears of Theory: International Relations as Storytelling
   Sungju Park-Kang
Creative Methods in Military Studies
   Edited by Alice Cree
The Self, and Other Stories: Being, Knowing, Writing
   Laura J. Shepherd
Ripping, Cutting, Stitching: Feminist Knowledge Destruction and Creation in Global Politics
   Shine Choi, Michelle Brown, Cristina Masters, Swati Parashar, Saara Särmä, and Marysia Zalewski

The Self, and Other Stories

Being, Knowing, Writing

Laura J. Shepherd

ROWMAN & LITTLEFIELD
Lanham • Boulder • New York • London

Published by Rowman & Littlefield
An imprint of The Rowman & Littlefield Publishing Group, Inc.
4501 Forbes Boulevard, Suite 200, Lanham, Maryland 20706
www.rowman.com

86-90 Paul Street, London EC2A 4NE, United Kingdom

Copyright © 2023 by The Rowman & Littlefield Publishing Group, Inc.

All rights reserved. No part of this book may be reproduced in any form or by any electronic or mechanical means, including information storage and retrieval systems, without written permission from the publisher, except by a reviewer who may quote passages in a review.

British Library Cataloguing in Publication Information Available

Library of Congress Cataloging-in-Publication Data Available

ISBN 9781538169636 (cloth) I ISBN 9781538169643 (pbk.) I ISBN 9781538169650 (ebook)

Beloved: when you were born, all I could say, as I lay there exhausted and you were placed on my chest, was "There you are." Still today, here you are, and I do not take that for granted. It is a privilege to walk with you as you make sense for yourself of place, self, and being. Your courage is an inspiration. You are my heart.

Contents

Preface

Relax what you don't need.

I have been putting off writing this preface for weeks. Partly that is because I am currently in full-blown burnout and exerting any kind of creative energy is exhausting. I have always found it effortful to construct mental imagery, but for a long time now, I have held at the forefront of my mind a cartoonish representation of my depleted cognitive functions: a brain that is a mass of sluggish circuits and the sparking of frustrated disconnections, pulsing sickly and darkish purple instead of the Pepto-Bismol pink of a healthy cartoon brain. It is hard to marshal this tender bruise, to gently coax it into functioning effectively, even for a little while. Today I have walked in nature, breathed into gentle yoga poses, and taken a bath to soothe my dysregulated nervous system. I have woken from a nap, feeling perhaps it is possible to write, and here I am. But it is mostly not even the fatigue and the difficulty I am having marshaling my thoughts these days that has had me averting my eyes from my laptop when I walk into the kitchen where it is resting on the worktop. I have been invited to write a preface that explains why I wrote this book, what is the nature of its contribution, and who it is intended for—and the truth is that I am still not sure I have the answers to any of these questions.

Sometimes, this book feels like an inhalation. It is the sharp intake of breath that precedes an act of courage, or a confrontation, the short

panicky gasp that fills only the upper chest and brings an acute awareness of the blood pulsing in my body. I have a squirming feeling of
unease and discomfort when I consider letting it go. This is the bodily
knowing that it is not up to me to judge how this book fits, where this
book fits, if this book fits, in the constellation of all of the other books
to which we turn for inspiration, validation, and confirmation. It is the
holding of my breath at the top, the moment when, in fear or stress or
overwhelm, I forget to exhale. It is the accumulation of all the forgotten
exhalations of my academic life, and it makes me dizzy.

But this book also feels like a release. In some ways, I wrote this
book to see if I could. Or perhaps more accurately because I couldn't
not write this book any longer: before forming them here, I carried its
stories around with me for a lifetime in some cases, as much a part of
me as the scar at the base of my throat, the patterning of lines on my
hand that I see echoed on my child's palm, and the tension that has
accumulated in my right shoulder. I have lived these stories and they are
in, and of, me, and it is time to let them go. I need to release these stories
to make space for whatever comes next. I need to let them breathe; I
need them to let me breathe. I need to let this book go.

I am focusing on the breath at the moment because it is the thing that
grounds me, the simplest affirmation each day that I am still here. I can
always come back to my breath. I have been practicing yoga and breath-
work for a year or so now, a journey that has accompanied the journey
of this book into the world. As a result of my daily yoga practice, I
am learning to work in and with my body—not to chase sensation or
expect anything other than that I show up to my mat each morning, the
need for which has intensified with the physical symptoms of burnout.
Some days I fall over when I transition between poses. Some days it
is all I can manage to lie in child's pose, with my knees wide and my
forehead against the mat, sending a deep breath down my spine and
into my belly to reassure my nervous system that rest is possible. To
encourage breathing into each pose, one of my favorite YouTube yoga
teachers says, "*Relax what you don't need*," an advice I find infinitely
easier to follow than exhortations to simply "*Let go*." Perhaps she
recognizes that the people who have found her videos, people who are
learning to practice yoga from YouTube, need a little more help than
the average human in understanding letting go. When she says "*Relax
what you don't need*," I scan over my body, finding and breathing into
the inevitable knots and pockets of tension in my neck, shoulders, and

hips, until these areas soften. I am always surprised at how much more there is to exhale. This book surprised me too.

Writing this book has been an ongoing reminder to bring the fullness of each breath, the wholeness of my humanity, into my work. The chapters are grounded in, and mostly inspired by, the experience of the ways in which we are encouraged to express being and knowing in the contemporary academy. I have written these chapters not only to make myself visible in the work but also to make the overarching point that knowledge production in the social sciences might look different if we could create and hold space for different ways of writing (and being and knowing). This point is both central and incidental to the book, in that it is not proffered as an "argument" as such; the chapters cohere only loosely around the idea that the disciplining practices which produce our limited modes of academic expression can be encountered otherwise. Each chapter is a stand-alone piece of writing, but the themes and motifs to which I return in each encourage reflection on academic subjectification across the interconnected spaces we both inhabit and produce.

Finally, I run my tongue over my teeth and wonder for whom I write, wonder why I write my self into being on these pages, and wonder how I justify taking up this space. As a colleague observed, mine is the story of a middle-class white woman. *"I am not sure we need another story like that."* That colleague is undoubtedly correct. I feel awkward, and deeply ambivalent, about taking up space in this way, space in an environment that is still so inhospitable to so many. And yet I am here, writing. Because I am, and am not, the story. I exist alongside, in parallel, or surfacing in traces and echoes. I strive to be the vehicle for the story, rather than the story itself. Perhaps I am just the expression; perhaps my worlds are the subject. This book both—inevitably—is and is not about me, my self, my "I" self. It is just the quiet inhalation and exhalation of the breath. It is me learning, finally, to relax what I don't need. To let go.

Laura J. Shepherd
Sydney, Australia
August 31, 2022

Acknowledgments

Most of the work on this book was supported by an Australian Research Council Future Fellowship research grant (2018–2022, grant ID 170100037). I am extremely grateful for the opportunities afforded by this award.
Two chapters of the book are lightly edited versions of essays that were previously published as stand-alone articles:

Chapter 3, "Encounter," was previously published as: "Research as Gendered Intervention: Feminist Research Ethics and the Self in the Research Encounter," *Crítica Contemporánea: Revista de Teoría Política*, 2016, No. 6.

Chapter 4, "Engagement," was previously published as: "Activism in/and the Academy: Reflections on 'Social Engagement,'" *Journal of Narrative Politics*, 2018, 5(1).

Other bits and pieces of the text throughout started out, or have appeared, as parts of blog posts (with special thanks to The Disorder of Things, for hosting my ramblings over the years), unpublished conference papers, and emails to friends and colleagues. Certain passages have been improved immeasurably, having been shared in draft form with some of those same friends and colleagues and then revised. I am profoundly grateful in particular to Roxani Krystalli, Nicole Wegner, and Spike Peterson, all of whom have been generous with insights, companionship, and care over the past few years.

The cover art is an image titled "Ink on Skin," which seemed appropriate. I am grateful to Reddit user RightyHoThen for permission to use it here.

Chapter 1

Exegesis

I bring the cold in with me, along with faint traces of humidity, the surprising warmth of the tenacious Australian winter sun, and the smoke haze of back-burning, somewhere close but a world away from this sandstone monument to settler colonial ideas about civilization and the custodianship of knowledge. I still feel new here, relatively, and yet I know this place, and it knows me. It is in me, it has formed me, without my understanding and without my conscious consent. It seems inevitable somehow that I would be here, in this office, this morning, distracted by the dull hum of the fan, writing.

There is a part of me that is always writing. I'm not sure I even know who I am when I'm not writing. Whether I grasp and flail for expressions that elude me, or whether the words tumble onto the page joyfully, writing completes me. This understanding pulls me out of bed at 3:00 a.m. to the blue light of my laptop in the dark; I trust my need to pour out the flow of words from my busy anxious brain to the curated presentation of my life in letters. In the elaboration of her own encounters with autoethnography, Elizabeth Dauphinee explains that she writes out of love, out of guilt, out of anger, sleeplessness, or aggravation, though in all cases out of an abiding sense "that something is not the way I thought it was".[1] These words nestle deep in the space beneath my heart

---

[1] Elizabeth Dauphinee, "The Ethics of Autoethnography," *Review of International Studies*, 2010, 36(4): 799–818, p.808.

and fit comfortably there; they were already part of me—the part of me
that makes sense of my self and my worlds through my writing.

I toggle between windows, drafting

Hey, are we ok?

$4 => y+1$ *mentions, does that make sense?*

Dear Isabella,
Thank you for the report, and for your time last week. I

I what? I am lost. I still my busy hands and feel the cold on the tips of
my fingers. I can't explain. I can't finish that sentence. I go back to the
previous email: "If it would be easier to fix a time a chat, that is fine and
welcome." It would be easier for me. So much easier to think about how
to explain to my brilliant colleague how I think we could organize the
database we're building than to think about how to write to the woman
who has become our family psychologist.

Dear Isabella,
I wonder whether it would be possible to schedule a time to discuss

The distractions of the database, the emails, and the possibility of a
chat are all fine and welcome, and right now on this cool bright April
day they are distractions; despite the fact that it's 9:40 a.m. on a Monday and they absolutely should be my focus, my priority, they are not.
My priority is the email that I can't write, the conversations that I can't
work out how to have, the people in and of my world. My priority
now, always, is the relations that hold me, the communities that nourish and sustain me, but the tendrils of connections that I send out from
my desk to theirs are a way of navigating this exhausting and endlessly
complicated life. Even when it feels impossible, I write those connections into being, write them strong—is it courage or a different kind of
fear that allows me to put these feelings into words?—and write them,
and me, out into the world. I am, you are, we are, made of these words.
   We are all many stories, and there are many stories here. Most of
them—parts of all of them—are not mine to tell. I have struggled endlessly with this ethical dilemma, as I perceive it, struggled to make
sense of how much and who and when and whether to let my worlds
collide on and with these pages.

After all, our stories are not our own. In the process of writing about ourselves, we invariably write about others. And in this act we run the risk of making those we write about not only recognisable to others but recognisable to themselves in ways they might not feel comfortable with or agree to even if they have given their informed consent (whatever this might mean) for the story to be told.[2]

Mostly those are conversations that I do not want to have, that I do not know how to have. How to explain to my friends that our laughter is now foiled for my reflections, to my child that the set of their bottom lip in discomfort is now mine to account for and interweave with stories of databases and desperation?

In an earlier draft of this chapter, which spawned its ghost twin, I expanded on the email that I cannot write.

Dear Isabella,

As I wrote and rewrote this chapter, I grew less and less comfortable with the words that originally followed these. There was too much in the telling, a lifetime in a paragraph of uncertainty and restlessness and grating frustration. A person imprisoned in that paragraph, immobilized in my words, presented here without consent or consultation for the advancement of my story. I highlighted those words in red, and they bloodied me every time I turned to this section. I told myself I had to excise them, a surgical removal. I refused. I cried. I was committed to the pain I had written, to honoring that story, which was *mine*. At least, it felt like mine. But imagining this book in your hands, imagining this book in the hands of those whom I love most dearly, those for whom I would unhesitatingly hold out my heart, imagining their feeling of betrayal at my recounting that which was presumed privileged, safe, locked away—that imagining erased me as I eventually erased the words I couldn't carry in my soul. There are words, it turns out, with which I cannot reconcile, but these words are parts of me too.

This deliberation stalled my writing for many months. I have tried to make peace with the violence of this form; turning again to Dauphinee, I tried to find my way to understand that this kind of writing

---

[2] Andrew Sparkes, "Autoethnography at the Will of the Body: Reflections on a Failure to Produce in Time," 203–211 in Nigel P. Short, Lydia Turner and Alec Grant, eds, *Contemporary British Autoethnography* (Rotterdam: Sense) 2013, p.207.

is not an appropriation of others (at least not any greater in terms of its violence than the academic voice, which pounds others into manageable interview materials), but rather a reflexive awareness of the self as a perpetrator of a certain kind of violence in the course of all writing and all representation.[3]

I feel that violence, and I have intellectualized its defense, its justification. I have expounded on the violence of fixity of meaning, of partiality and paucity and impossibility of representation, and suppressed the slightly sick feeling that rises when I know that even I am not quite buying the story I am trying to sell. So I have tried but failed to turn from violence here, to abdicate the culpability I feel in revealing the hidden lives of all my others. I am held in relation to all these others and I owe them care; their stories are not mine, as much as my stories are not my own. But in the space between us, I nurture an ethical attachment, an ethical obligation, which can become the quality of those relations. I write and hope to do right by the people whose lives intersect with mine. I carry that hope, the outer shining edges of the squirming acknowledgment that all autoethnographic writing (all writing, perhaps) is extractive and violent, and match it with the obligation that falls on all researchers to "get the story right" and "tell the story well."[4]

Too often I navigate between the Scylla of arrogant detachment and Charybdis of total dissolution and even with care as my guide I am undone. I feel not that care protects me but that it plagues me, a cause of dis-ease; I am infected with care for those with whom I am held in relation and this erases me. I forget how to hold myself together, to contain myself, and to take responsibility only for what is mine. I am learning to articulate my need for integration, and how much more grounded I feel when I admit my boundedness—to recognize that *we* is not a zero-sum calculation but that *I* is not infinite. The care that I

[3] Dauphinee, "The Ethics of Autoethnography," 799–818, p.806.
[4] Linda Tuhiwai Smith, *Decolonizing Methodologies: Research and Indigenous Peoples*, 2nd edn. (London: Zed Books) 2012, p.226. Smith is talking specifically about the egregious epistemic violence perpetrated against Indigenous people in (settler-)colonial research practices and the responsibility of researchers to center Indigenous voices and ways of being, knowing, and doing in the construction of knowledge about Indigenous people. I am neither seeking to draw any equivalence here between mine and Smith's work nor to suggest that this book contributes in any meaningful way to efforts toward decolonizing research, but many of the ethical dimensions of representation in research that Smith explores are relevant to (auto)ethnography.

carry with me gives rise to a relational ethic, which honors the need "to advance critical thought which does not deny the multiplicity and wildness of our interrelated selves."[5] These are the condition of this book's possibility. These are the conditions of which I write and the conditions of my writing.

* * *

My words and worlds are not mine alone, even as I am centered here: the *auto* in autoethnography. Much of the literature on autoethnography in my discipline dances around the idea that there is something profoundly self-indulgent about centering the self in stories about world politics,[6] about centering the self at all. This charge is one that makes the back of my mouth taste of metal, makes my skin prickle, and my heart hurt. This is the undercurrent of shame that runs throughout this book, perhaps throughout my life. I have behaved badly, been careless, and made poor choices in many situations, and I am ashamed of these moments, a shame that is not remediated even as I open them up for consideration in these pages or in my own deliberations and rememberings. Fear compounds this shame to produce something related but different, a shame that seeks to shrink and diminish, that folds in on itself and demands self-effacement rather than situating the self as the focus of analytical scrutiny. This toxic shame whispers that any effort will never be enough, but simultaneously that any effort is always too much, more than is deserved. Writing autoethnography, it turns out, is an exercise in holding space for contradiction, for multiplicity—for the tension and the release, the inhalation and the exhalation of each breath.

Autoethnography. I turn the word over in my mouth. I am a dilettante etymologist, I love the idea that words bear traces of language used and reused and reconfigured over time. Central to the craft (the art? the science?) of self-people-writing is the relationships, the connectivity of self with people with writing, which resonates with me on a deep frequency indiscernible to my consciousness. My self and the complicated messy life I have and that I share with my people matters in and to and

---

[5] Sarah Amsler and Sara C. Motta, "The Marketized University and the Politics of Motherhood," *Gender and Education*, 2019, 31(1): 82–99, p.88.

[6] An exemplary exposition of this concern is provided in: Sarah Naumes, "Is all 'I' IR?" *Millennium: Journal of International Studies*, 2015, 43(3): 820–832.

bleeds on IR. I write to weave my world together, to order and connect and make whole my own experience.

I have tried, and failed, to write this book over the past few years. These words, the translation of life into experience told—its narration—have clamored for my attention; in the darkness of anxious morning hours, as I walk, as I knit to pacify restless fingers, as I exist, this book has stalked me. These words are a bruise that my touch skitters over, around, away from, but the tenderness has an appeal I can't understand, an appeal which exceeds my ability to focus on the other thing, all the other things, and I find myself opening these files almost furtively and nailing these butterflies to the wall. This book has spilled over me and at times it is like drinking from an over-pressured hosepipe in a moment of desperate thirst; I am helpless and gulping at the relief the water brings but it hurts. This book has confronted me and found me wanting, for "What expert am I?"[7]

---

[7] Dauphinee, "The Ethics of Autoethnography," 799–818, p.802. In the section I have quoted here, Dauphinee explores the grounds on which we stand as academic when we write of the pain and violence endured by others, reflecting on the question of expertise posed to her by Stojan Sokolović, a survivor of the war on which she has "built [a] career" (p.802). The account of that question in the pages that follow is one of the best elaborations of how we fail to encounter the worlds that we are notionally trying to understand that I have read, and it stays with me as something of a touchstone for my own narrative work:

> It [the question of expertise] charged me with faithlessness writ large, with an inescapable responsibility, to which I could simply make no adequate response. It asked me not with which experts I had spoken, or what they had said. It asked me not what scraps of truth were contained on the tiny little audiocassettes that comprised my burgeoning library of interview archives. It asked, instead, if I had noticed the slant of the setting sun on the terracotta tiles of the rooftops. It asked me if I had stuck my fingers in the honeycomb brickwork of the buildings along the Vrbas River or run the flat palm of my hand along the stuccoed gypsum plaster of the borrowed house in which I slept. It asked me if I had endured the rain at an inopportune moment, or if I had even noticed the rain at all—if I had divined anything in it. It asked me what the future held as read through the dried coffee grounds on the bottom of my cup. It asked me, to put it differently, if I had thought of something other than what I had been trained to look for. And in so doing, it asked me if there was even a possibility of narrative truth—whether anyone could actually apprehend, process, signify, and render it in speech or text or microform. The questions that presupposed the form (if not the content) of acceptable answerability were obliterated in that single sentence—what expert are you?—asked rhetorically, perhaps, because there was no possibility of making answer along the lines for which my training had prepared me (p.803).

The question of disciplinary training—of becoming and unbecoming disciplined—is entirely bound up in the work I am trying to do in this book, and it is probably the reason that this love letter to Dauphinee's setting sun and honeycomb brickwork is buried in a footnote rather than centered in the text. Perhaps I am concerned that I have nothing more to add to the consideration of this question; perhaps this question is all there is, for any of us: "What expert are you?"

This book proposes that I am—or can be, or perhaps one day might be—at least able to give an account of my self, among other things. This is my exegesis, my extended interpretation of academic life, conventions, and practices through which I stumble toward understanding that life, those conventions and practices, and their generative and stultifying effects. This is a project that

> conceives of the individual not just as an interpreter of social reality, but as someone who can understand her/himself through thinking about social institutions, practices, and phenomena. . . . I seek to understand how my own subjectivity was constituted by the international: meaning, both by academic IR theory and by international political practices and institutions.[8]

This is a project that turns my analytical lens, honed through twenty years of training and learning and mimicry and error, on my self and presents my findings in the form of an autoethnographic narrative, a series of loosely connected chapters and vignettes that weaves together recollection, reflection, and revelation. I present here my self, and other stories.

I have, of course, always been present in the stories I have told. Every piece of "academic" writing, published in learned journals or in book form, bears more or less visible traces of me; I am a palimpsest always there for discovery. I write not only to be visible but politically to *have visibility*: I write always against the erasure of my self from those pages because the inoculation of science from infection by the self—by *care*—is how the idea that we are not present in our work perpetuates. More than this, however, I write myself into being in and through these "academic" texts just as I do in this narrative style. Rotate the world a quarter-turn and all are fictions, of sorts. I am comfortable with fiction, with being/telling stories.[9]

There is no doubt in my mind that what I am writing here is fiction, at least in part. From the Latin *fingere*, to form or contrive, I derive comfort

---

[8] Oded Löwenheim, "The 'I' in IR: An Autoethnographic Account," *Review of International Studies*, 2010, 36(4): 1023–1045, p.1025.

[9] Annick Wibben explains that our humanity is in part defined by our storytelling drive and capacity: we are "*homo fabulans*," she offers, both telling and interpreting the world through stories. Annick T. R. Wibben, *Feminist Security Studies: A Narrative Approach* (London and New York, NY: Routledge) 2011, p.43.

from writing my self as fiction. This is an imaginative enterprise, a process of making and unmaking the self through my writing, of hiding and
seeking and re-presenting my experiences and encounters. My self does
not exist fully formed, beneath sediment, to be excavated and exhibited;
I am invented in these pages but that does not make me un*true*. For
me, the fiction of the self is both target and production of this critical
interrogation. So I want to confound the juxtaposition between writing
fiction—deliberately, provocatively, and creatively—and writing autobi-
ography or memoir; some want to hold on to fiction writing as a form,[10]
some to disregard it, but what of the fiction that is already the (integrated,
knowing) self? Setting fiction against non-fiction writing in International
Relations as a mode of explanation and encounter not only presumes a
level of investment from the field that I am not convinced exists but also
erases for me the question of how the "I" that writes is constituted, if not
as a fiction, a figment, a chimera. In my writing, I am (un)done. Thus I
am not proposing a "constructive dialogue"[11] between those seeking to
write fiction and those clinging fast to facts but a different configuration
of the matter, a different configuration of the (writing) self entirely.

* * *

We moved en masse, often, in my graduate program. Through seminar
rooms, to the gardens behind the Politics Department where we smoked
furiously and distracted ourselves from the pain of producing double-
spaced pages of mostly substandard work, to the pubs within walking
distance from the university where we continued to smoke, and drink too
much, and talk about what we'd read, and what we hadn't written, and
our small dreams. Sometimes it feels like we had a collective consciousness; certainly, my two closest friends in the program and I were referred
to as "the three." It was exclusionary and awful and I loved it, because
it was the first time in a long time I had felt anything like belonging.

So I don't know who was present, exactly, when one of the academic
staff said bluntly "I've been asked to talk to you about your clothes." I know
where we were: we were in the pub, and there were near-empty glasses on
the table, and there were three, or five, or more of us there, and I had felt it

---

[10] Sungju Park-Kang, "Fictional IR and Imagination: Advancing Narrative Approaches,"
Review of International Studies, 2015, 41(2): 361–381.
[11] Park-Kang, "Fictional IR and Imagination," p.369.

was our regular swarm but then I looked around and recognized that it was just us women who were being talked to about our clothes. My stomach clenched, and I tasted shame and cheap white wine at the back of my throat. I can't pretend to remember the conversation in detail, this reprimand that was delivered probably twenty years ago now, but I can remember how it felt—how it felt to be told that wearing sleeveless tops in summer or racer-back T-shirts was *unprofessional*. How it was *distracting*. How we wanted to be *taken seriously*. How no one was going to take us seriously if they could see our bra straps. I poured more wine, tucked away the hurt and the betrayal, and nodded in agreement that I, more than anything, wanted to be taken seriously.

The first international academic conference I attended was in San Diego, USA, in 2006. I asked my supervisor what I should wear. "A suit," she told me, so I asked my mum to buy me a suit for my birthday, which fortuitously fell the month before the conference. I loved that suit. It had a neat, fitted jacket and a pencil skirt and it was somewhere between dark tan and the color of old copper before it turns green, and it was a little on the small side but that was okay because I didn't have enough money to eat three meals a day during the conference anyway. I bought a banana and a soft pretzel at the gas station each day on the way from our budget accommodation to the conference site, along with a large coffee, and I made the food last through till dinner. I made sure no one could see my bra straps, and even when I was perched awkwardly and alone on the edge of a sun-lounger by a swimming pool that none but the most fearless—or foolish—were using, I felt good. I was uncomfortable, anxious, and terrified of saying the wrong thing all the time, and I thought that this was how academia was supposed to feel.

As I sit here writing about bra straps and pretzels, I am grinding my teeth, not only at the prospect of having to make sense of these complicated feelings about my academic self but because I still feel that I am circling around the whole of which this is a part: this book, this story, these words. These words lay my self bare, picking at wounds scabbed over but still tender, connecting the shoreline walks that ground me with the imperatives of the academy. I have pretended for many months that I don't have time to finish this book at the moment—and it's true, in one sense, I am living a lot of life at present—but the truth is that I am scared. This book reveals much more than my bra straps, and don't I still want to be taken seriously?

This book is borne of privilege. It is a deliberate turning away from my academic home and training, which itself is enabled by the wash

and waves of my career to this point. I will probably be forgiven if this
ill-disciplined account of my self is a tragic and awful disaster, and if I
am not, if the retreat of the waves leaves detritus at my feet rather than
smooth sand on which to start anew, I suspect I will struggle to care. I feel
unbounded, untamed, and connected to this project in a way that I have
missed as I have failed and labored with others, and I am writing this book
because I want to, not because I feel I should. But still, it terrifies me.

Roxanne Doty's words are a balm and a gift as I sit with this uneasy
rebellion. She says:

> The imperatives of "the discipline" and the academy more broadly to write
> in a certain voice are very powerful and sometimes difficult to escape. This
> issue would not hold the importance that it does for me, had I not person-
> ally experienced the "discipline of the discipline," the slow often unnotice-
> able slipping away of my own voice into an abyss of academic jargon.[12]

Perhaps I write to retrieve my voice from the tides, or perhaps only
now do I recognize that my voice is carried on the tides, to the far blue
horizon I can see through my kitchen window, to which my attention
wanders but is forgiven for it nourishes me in ways I cannot quite
understand. When I walk in the shallows of the ocean, I hear my soul
whisper. When writing, I whisper back in recognition, and my words
are footprints in the sand.

* * *

There are imperatives in the academy that still drive me. I am overwhelmed with grief when I read yet another Twitter thread or email
about the exploitation of precariously and contingently employed
colleagues, of researchers starting out whose ideas are appropriated
and whose maltreatment at the hands of more experienced researchers
breaks their hearts and spirits and drives them from these spaces con-
figured to and for them as inhospitable. I am impelled to act against, to
counterbalance, these forces as best I can; again, this is borne of privilege. But simultaneously I am implicated in the reproduction of these

---

[12] Roxanne Lynn Doty, "Maladies of Our Souls: Identity and Voice in the Writing of Academic International Relations," *Cambridge Review of International Affairs*, 2004, 17(2):
377–392, pp.379–380.

dynamics; this is not a heroic tale, and I slay no dragons here. Yes, I can work against silence; I can amplify and lift up and create space and hold on but I am always benefiting from the structures that I challenge, even in the choice I have made to write in this register. "[P]ersonal narrative can actively be used as a tool of silencing which works to reinforce the power of the dominant through capitalising upon emotional responses and invisibilising structural dynamics."[13] There is no purity of heart, no good intention, that can save the valiant protagonist from being conditioned by their environment; plaudits and awards are my shields and my disguise and I don them gratefully to dodge and parry the threats of my unveiling, of my own precarity. For the precarity that we share in the venture of "knowledge production" in the neoliberal academy, the "marketized university," is not shared equally, and I nudge others forward, closer to the edge, as I myself retreat.

Acknowledging my complicity is essential to my exploration of the academic world I inhabit, and essential to this form; "rather than some self-indulgent attempt to insulate oneself from critique, autoethnography must instead open the self to that critique."[14] In fact, I am less sure of my ability to insulate myself from critique, from the scratchy inner reviewer that judges and finds wanting my movements and morals. I am learning to sit with the manifold and spectacular catastrophes of my life to this point, with the devastation of my "lost decade," as I refer to it wryly, hoping that the evident self-deprecation will blunt the critical edge of my own self-hatred, to sit with the catastrophes of my mid-teens to my mid-twenties rather than slide past them in denial or guilt or shame. I am learning, in the words of Maya Angelou, that I did then what I knew how to do. Now that I know better, I do better. Or at least I try. And part of my complicity in this system is the debt I owe, because I think I might not have made it through to the end of my lost decade at all were it not for the academy. This is how I have come to know my self, to learn my self, and I question whether in another life I would have survived at all. Small wonder then that I have learned to reflect on learning, to reflect on knowing, and being, and to consider, still "what expert am I?" How did I (do I) find myself here and how does the here in which I find myself shape me? What, and how, can I know (of) my self?

---

[13] Alison Phipps, "Whose Personal is More Political? Experience in Contemporary Feminist Politics," *Feminist Theory* 17(3): 303–321, p.307.
[14] Dauphinee, "The Ethics of Autoethnography," 799–818, p.810.

And so, here I am, writing. Writing to learn, to know. "Knowing is not so much about the assemblage of existing knowledge as it is about recognizing our constitution as 'ourselves' within the fragments that we process as knowledge."[15] I am working away from fragments, toward integration, in the half-light of the afternoon. And I have learned that this is how I integrate. This is how I become, through story—stories of, and are, my (un)doing.

> The story does not simply describe, it demands representation outside itself. Indeed, the story cannot tell itself without our willingness to imagine what it cannot tell. The story asks that we live with what cannot be explained. . . . The story opens the door to curiosity; the reams of evidence dissipate as we tell the world differently, with creative precision.[16]

I have learned to be curious through my writing, to tell my worlds differently, and to consider what, and how, I know, as illusory, shifting, painfully small. Perhaps, I am what cannot be explained.

* * *

I have read a lot, and written a little, about ethics in research practice, exploring what it means to extend ethical obligation in and through my research encounters, and this is fine and well, but there is so much more to ethics than this. So much more than can be captured or contained within applications for approval from the Human Research Ethics Committee of my institution, so much more even than can inform my discussions with my students and the participants in my research alike. The currents of ethical practice run through my engagement with my work, at once superficial and undertow, drowning me in eddies of accountability and care and shame. There is no way to *do* ethics, to *be* ethical, I might as well try to catch the light on water. Yet I deliberate on what I owe, on the relations in which I am held, and on my responsibilities.

There is a prior discussion to have with students and research participants alike, before ethical approval can be sought or granted, about

---

[15] Avtar Brah, "The Scent of Memory: Strangers, Our Own, and Others," *Feminist Review*, 1999, 61: 4–26, p.5.

[16] Katherine McKittrick, *Dear Science and Other Stories* (Durham, NC: Duke University Press) 2021, p.7. It would feel dishonest not to acknowledge that McKittrick's intervention specifically related to Black and anticolonial methodologies. I pick up on this discomfort, my own discomfort with appropriating storytelling as a craft, in chapter 5.

Ethics (light on water). Photo by author.

the ludicrous pretense that ethical obligation can be discharged: secure consent; avoid sensitive subjects; approve transcripts before analysis; approve attribution before publication. Tick, tick, tick. This is ethics-by-numbers, which is only fractionally about being humans engaged together in the pursuit of connection, understanding, and insight. And it has no relevance here in any case. How do I lay bare my ethics when I am the subject of my inquiry? How do I secure consent when every glance and chance encounter, meaningful and frivolous conversation, and hour spent in cafés or conference rooms, has formed and informed me and the world I examine here? And what of my obligation to myself? How can I ensure protection and mitigate against "reputational harm," when I have singularly failed, for most of my life, to take myself seriously as an entity deserving of care, of compassion? These encounters leave me hollow and breathless some days but still I am committed to this project, this *exegesis*.

So, in this examination I hold myself to account, but more than that, I wish to welcome—wholeheartedly be open to—being held to account by those who care, with whom I am in relation, and that is part of navigating this form. I consider the fear of indulgence and wonder what is driving colleagues—and me—to equate self-revelation with excess. Again, I am always already in and of my research, my writing. I am here. Perhaps I am no longer apologizing for my presence. Perhaps giving this account, and thus honoring the various threads and ties of accountability, is an act of recalibration, of repositioning my center—an occupation of space.

I was profoundly bulimic and frequently anorexic for almost twenty years. I tell people it was ten years, to coincide neatly with my lost decade, but it was longer. It took longer to accept food as a source of nourishment and not trauma. It took longer to learn to hear my body, to eat when I was hungry, and stop when I was not. It took the longest time to accept the space I take up in the world, to feel able to be in that space without hesitation, and I am often not there, even now, but I know that place exists, and that's something. I am angry about the years I wasted on wasting time, food, and love. I am sad for fourteen-year-old me who had no better way to express the terror she felt in a world beyond her control than through restricting and counting and punishing her miserable self. I am sad for twenty-one-year-old me who scribbled in her therapeutically mandated journal.

> *This is the reality of an eating disorder. It's not a glamourous child-woman slowly fading into the background, it's a painfully skinny and perpetually cold half broken wretch sticking her fingers down her throat in the restaurant toilets and pretending to her friends waiting at the table that she's got a stomach upset while they pretend to believe her.*

I am sad for every me who turned such violence in on herself and who forced herself to believe that she was not lessened through her lessening, that she had to keep on.

> *I know the steps of this dance so well. Skip a meal or two, get hungry, get control. Get thin, get <u>really</u> thin. Get sick. Disappear.*

I live with the after-effects of almost twenty years of disordered eating, of course. I live with myriad pains and dysfunctions and the quiet echoes of the constant self-critical voice. I have a healthier relationship with food now, though my loved ones still look at me sideways on occasion, especially when I announce another food I'm having to cut out of my diet because it triggers migraine, stomach pain, or other kinds of bodily stress. I blame myself, and it is frustrating. In conversation with my therapist last year, I realized that my tendency to deal with stress at work by working more is driven by the same impulse that governed my relationship with eating for so many years: both hyper-productivity and denial of basic nourishment are, for me, about needing to be good-better-perfect. I am learning that good enough is good enough.

This experience has changed the way I feel about responsibility. I am responsible for what I did, and what I do, and I invite accountability. But again turning to Maya Angelou: now I know better, I do better. By myself, certainly, and probably by others, with whom I can be more honest, to whom I can be more connected, among whom I can move and laugh and be, not without trepidation but with less, at least. Translating this to scholarship opens up the possibility of responsible scholarship, ethical scholarship, being that which admits to the whole humanity of a person. The whole humanity of a person is engaged in meaning-making, and we do that—*I* do that—in and through these reflections.

My whole personhood is re-presented here, but I am a precarious fiction. Writing this project, in this way, is a way of excavating my foundations, of establishing my self, and *here* and *I* and *am*. There is no closure to be sought here but none to be expected. After all

> The stable closure of the tale is only false in the sense that all stories are tales because they only selectively mimic—re-present—the events they are about. The important thing is that they be good enough for the moment, that they allow us to keep on loving into the senselessness of actual life and somehow, miraculously, transubstantiate it into something meaningful.[17]

And so, here I am, writing. Smoothing my self in words and making meaning as I go. I write to know myself and, through myself, worlds.

---

[17] Patrick T. Jackson, "Three Stories," 161–172 in Naeem Inayataullah, ed. *Autobiographical International Relations: I, IR* (London: Routledge) 2011, p.172.

Chapter 2

Expertise

PART 1: PEDAGOGUE

Parker Palmer proposes that teaching always occurs at "the dangerous intersection of personal and public life."[1] I am momentarily captured by the idea of a dangerous intersection, and I permit myself a few moments of wonder about the sounds and the lights and the metallic taste of heavy traffic in the night and the vulnerability of a human body at another kind of dangerous intersection. I smile in wry acknowledgment that this thought path is equivalent to my child's insistence that a different pencil (because the scratchiness of graphite on paper is at times overwhelming and unbearable), or a drink of water (because a thirsty child cannot be reasonably expected to concentrate on long division), or a particular fidget toy (because it will help with concentration rather than act a distraction, most of the time—apart from when it acts as a distraction rather than helping with concentration) will be the thing that enables them to begin their homework assignment for the week. My homework assignment for the week is to write this chapter, and here I am, caught by the visualization of busy city streets and moving no further, with my thoughts or my imagined efforts to safely navigate the

---

[1] Part 1 of this essay was originally drafted for a roundtable at the International Studies Association annual convention in Toronto, Canada, in 2019. The roundtable convenors, Patrick Jackson and Andrea Paras, asked us to work with Parker Palmer's book, *The Courage to Teach*, as a thinking prompt. Parker Palmer, *The Courage to Teach: Exploring the Inner Landscape of a Teacher's Life* (San Francisco, CA: Jossey-Bass Publishers) 1998, p.18.

intersection I have conjured—much more consideration given to this metaphor than Palmer surely ever intended.

But I have grown used to the strange elliptical meandering that happens as my writing-self settles to a rhythm and a story. The subject of this story is teaching, but the subject is also me, which is fitting, because the subject that I am is (re)produced in the subject that I teach: I am not divisible from my "objects of study," nor can my claim to "subject matter expertise"—the "command of content that always eludes our grasp"[2]—be separated from my self-subject, given how invested I am in my academic identity. As Parker Palmer suggests, "the things I teach are things I care about—and what I care about helps define my selfhood."[3] So this is a story about subject knowledge, playing shamelessly with the idea of "the subject" to explore how we know (who we are) and how we (relate to what we) teach. It is also a story about courage, or rather, a story about teaching in conversation with courage, held by courage, and inspired to connect courage to danger (we are back to the intersection), fear, vulnerability, and—perhaps—hope.

What can I teach? What—and when—do I have the courage to teach? There is a presumption, in higher education at least, that I can teach what I know. I mostly feel that I know very little, and that actually the subjects that I know "best"—as if it were possible to qualitatively or even quantitatively measure how deep or profound is my understanding of a phenomenon or issue—are the hardest subjects to teach, those which take the most courage somehow. On those subjects, I trip myself up constantly, taking for granted too much in the knowledge-scape of my interlocutors because the acronyms I have learned to conjure with are alien to them, the actors I invoke to populate my scenes of contestation and compromise unknown, the dates that are as unforgettable to me as the birthdays of beloved friends do not signify to those with whom I speak in the same way. I talk in circles, forgetting, remembering, clarifying—confusing. I do not teach well, necessarily, when I teach these subjects, because it is a little like trying to teach someone about the sharp edge of the molar on the upper right side of my mouth, or the ache in my right knee joint when I sit cross-legged for too long. When I teach those subjects, I am trying to teach too far, reach too far back into and across my own history.

---

[2] Palmer, *The Courage to Teach*, p.2.
[3] Palmer, *The Courage to Teach*, p.17.

My knowledge of those subjects is in me, it *is* me. I have studied those subjects for two decades. That knowledge is in the growth and change of my body over those two decades: it is in the flattening of my feet through the pregnancy from which I delivered my child. It is in the muscles in my legs that I have developed and toned through running—early in the morning, in the midday sun, in the evening dodging commuters and mad cyclists and dog walkers in my local park—that I took up begrudgingly on advice from a coach who said I needed a way to make time for myself. It is no doubt in the ulcer with which I was mis-diagnosed in 2018, in the repetitive strain injury that needles me unforgivingly when I spend too long in front of my computer, in the choice to have my nose pierced as a very small claim to being untamed. But we do not often chart these ways of knowing when we—if we—recognize at all that bodies know. And I certainly cannot teach from these ways of knowing. At least, I don't think I can.

But can I teach the subjects that I don't know? Far greater in scope than can be adequately accounted for by the meager phrase "outside my area of expertise," the subjects that I cannot teach are innumerable, and the process of thinking about them too close to painful in its confrontation of endless wells of ignorance and limitation. But not-knowing is also freedom. Not-knowing a subject allows me to engage unfettered, unencumbered by the heavy mantel of expectation that rests upon those who presume to know (the "experts" I have written about elsewhere in this book). There is a lightness, a curiosity, an exuberance that comes from teaching the not-known subject. But it also means inhabiting the subject of not-knower, which is its own challenge, its own provocation. So much of the relationship in higher education between teacher and learner, teaching and learning, is dependent on—or at least shaped by—the presumed authority of the knowing subject, the known subject matter. (So much, of course, is dependent on—or at least shaped by—the process of undoing that presumed authority, subverting that relationship.) The abdication of the subject-position, the willingness to let the subject freefall—is this courage (to teach)? (And here, the plurality of subject as a noun is doing excellent work for me.)

Knowledge is enacted, neither revealed through careful investigation nor innate to and corroborated by the social world.[4] Teaching is

---

[4] I enjoy "enactment," which I have borrowed from Claudia Aradau and Jef Huysmans. See Claudia Aradau and Jef Huysmans, "Assembling Credibility: Knowledge, Method and Critique in Times of 'Post-Truth'," *Security Dialogue*, 2019, 50(1): 40–58, p.41.

a performance, one such mode of enactment, and as a subject I am interpellated in/through my teaching: knowledgeable, knowing, known. I go back to student evaluations of my teaching from courses in which I have taught the not-known subject (when I have felt the not-knowing subject): "She knows her stuff"; "exceptional knowledge"; "extensive knowledge"; "depth of knowledge"; "incredible knowledge"; "very knowledgeable." I have successfully passed as a knower, it seems. But how do they know what I know? I have produced knowledge in my performance of the knowing subject, but I have also produced—reproduced, really—security, even certainty, in first my understanding and now the understanding that my students express (feel). They know, because I know. They are as invested in my knowing as I am in theirs. But do we know together? Do they feel that they are knowers? And what other qualities do I bring to our encounter such that they accept my knowledge and see it as legitimate, deep, "extensive"?

Once again, I go back to the evaluations and I see myself through ungrammatical fragments of reflection from these people with whom I shared a semester or two. This teacher-me, this knower, is engaging, interesting, creative, energetic, and enthusiastic; she is accessible, passionate. "She clearly loves what she is doing." Love. Is that the right word? I often say that I love what I do: teaching, research, connecting people across institutions and territories, and building and sustaining a community, something I value. It is love; it "opens the heart,"[5] so it is risky. It brings fear. Love produces possibilities, while fear inhibits, it closes down, isolates, individuates, and limits. This is not the base instrumental fear of being unmasked as not-knower, but a deeper fear: a fear of destruction, of severing a connection or breaking something fragile that we as teacher-learners work on in the encounters that we share and that is necessarily a part of us/me. To love is to give of oneself. To teach is to give of oneself. To give is to be open, vulnerable (able to be wounded)—and "teaching is a daily exercise in vulnerability."[6]

Perhaps this is a space in which courage is required. We all of us come to the classroom with our prior knowledge, experience, commitments, and blind spots from the worlds that we inhabit, worlds that are,

---

[5] Palmer, *The Courage to Teach*, p.11.
[6] Palmer, *The Courage to Teach*, p.17.

in the words of Himadeep Muppidi, "distinctive and meaningful" to us.[7] I have to give up my distinctive and meaningful world when I teach, to open my self, my sense-making, my not-knowns, and my own "dangerous intersections." I have to encounter and be encountered, engage and be engaged. Learning happens in the spaces between those worlds, distinctive and meaningful as they are. Venturing between, reaching out across, those worlds takes courage. I am caught, in the pedagogical moment, in a prismatic relationship with so many selves and others, I scatter like light.[8] To trust at that moment, in the possibilities created by that depth of openness and vulnerability, that is where courage is needed.

Courage to teach. Fear to teach. Fear, to teach. I know that I can teach fear; I have been afraid. I have held my fragmented self together to survive and I have been shameless and shameful and afraid. Perhaps that is the source of both vulnerability and value. I know the skittery edge that dissonance brings to being in the classroom. That knowledge is still in my body, in sense-memories of cheap wine drunk twenty years ago to wash away the feeling of not-belonging, of being not-enough, not-right, not-knowing. I know that I can teach afraid; I have been fear. I have buried uncertainty and performed belonging and terrorized people who looked to me for reassurance that I couldn't provide. I did not know I was fearful, yet I knew. I did not know. I knew I did not know.

I try to make peace with knowledge. I smile to myself as I write that, because it is true in more than one way: in my research and teaching, I sometimes consider myself a scholar of peace. I believe that our words constitute our worlds, and I try to put more peace into the world than violence. But I also work against the abiding feeling of always not-knowing, teaching (being) a subject beyond my grasp. Knowledge is not my value. I feel conflicted, in conflict with knowledge and the forceful determination of the academy to make me a knowing subject yet deprive me of the space and the skill to learn how to subject myself to knowledge, to be at peace with being constructed through knowledge and my role in its (re)production. I write that I might better understand knowledge, how to know, what I know, and how I am known.

---

[7] Comments from a roundtable titled "Teaching Critical Thinking!? Strategies, Tools, and Methods," held at 58th Annual Convention of the International Studies Association in Baltimore, USA, 22–25 February 2017.
[8] This phrase is from Susanne Vega's "Small Blue Thing": "I Am Raining Down in Pieces/ I am Scattering Like Light" (1985).

Knowledge may not be my value, but it is my currency. I stand at the front of a lecture theater, or I sit at a table in a seminar room, or I quietly take a seat in a meeting room and I have bought entry to those spaces with my three gold coins: BA, MSc, PhD. I cannot be contained within those letters, but the legitimacy that accrues to me through the attainment of the right to append those letters to my signature if I wished to do so is equal to the skepticism with which I view them as markers of knowledge. And yet I trade in knowing. Perhaps this is because I continue to hope that I will indeed make peace with knowledge.

Hope is a tricky thing. I have an attachment to the configuration of "practicing hope" as a form of intellectual and/or academic politics,[9] and perhaps it is related to making peace with knowledge. The courage to teach is intimately—in textured and thrilling and disconcerting ways—related to hope, for me. I teach from fear, yes, but I also teach from hope. Hope is embedded in the way I make sense of the world. When my child was born, I realized I had never really known fear, responsibility, or vulnerability. My reaction to reading news of abuse or violation was amplified through the lens of this new attachment to create a new dimension of hurt. I was haunted by the generalized pain of knowing of an injury or loss and then the specific pain of imagining: how would I survive if that were my child? How could I live in a world without them in it? I used to go into their room at night and stand with my hand on their fragile back to witness their breath and feel the weight of the promise I had made to this small human when I brought them into this world.

There was never a conscious decision-making moment as far as I recall, but I did somehow come to the realization that I needed to find a way to cope with these fears, if they were not to overwhelm me (and therefore my child). In each moment, I chose (where I could) to *commit* hope, as a counterpoint to the commission of violence. This was not a vague resolution to "look on the bright side" or find the silver lining in every cloud but really a decision to practice hope in the face of extreme provocation, an insistence on thinking that we—as humans—are neither defined by the best nor the worst of our encounters and hoping

---

[9] I expand upon this in an interview with Elizabeth Dauphinee for the *Journal of Narrative Politics*. See Elizabeth Dauphinee and Laura J. Shepherd, "Editor's Interview with Laura J. Shepherd," *Journal of Narrative Politics*, 2016, 2(2): 105–116. Parts of this section draw on/from that interview.

that each of us will try to use our time here well, at least sometimes. I had to practice this feeling, hence my formulation of "practicing hope" (though the idea of "committing hope" also appeals). In a discipline defined by fear (per Neta Crawford's theorization),[10] practicing hope feels somewhat radical, and in a private life undone by the pain of others it was—is—transformative.

So I practice the courage to teach, yes, and I practice committing hope. "I am hopeful, not out of mere stubbornness, but out of an existential, concrete imperative."[11] I am stubborn, and yes, perhaps courageous, and I hope. "Without hope, what is left is *death*—the death of the spirit, the death of life—where there is no longer any sense of regeneration and renewal."[12] I try to make peace with knowledge. When I teach, I try to find courage to not-know, and to know, with the students with whom I share the encounter: to make connections and create new possibilities. These encounters are a generative practice, a living and lived experience, and hope is an integral part of that practice, for me.[13] Hope, even fluttering weakly, makes both knowing and not-knowing the subject bearable, as it opens the possibility of making/creating/generating something together, something possibly terrible but possibly new. I know hope, and hope is what impels me to try and know my self and subject.

PART 2: THREE MISTAKES

The slippery warm softness of the rice noodles was, in some way, what I was looking for in this bowl of broth, beef, and bok choi. I was looking for other things too, I think, under fluorescent lights in the cramped and teeming food court under the Hilton in Toronto in 2019: comfort, some residue or trace of home, as if a bowl of Toronto food court noodles could transport me across half a world to any one of the humid echoing

---

[10] Neta Crawford, "The Passion of World Politics: Propositions on Emotion and Emotional Relationships," *International Security*, 24(4): 116–156.

[11] Paulo Freire, *Pedagogy of Hope: Reliving Pedagogy of the Oppressed* (London: Bloomsbury) 2014, p.2.

[12] Mary Zournazi, *Hope: New Philosophies for Change* (Annandale: Pluto Press) 2002, p.16.

[13] I am deeply inspired by Naeem Inayatullah's reflections on pedagogy as encounter. Naeem Inayatullah, *Pedagogy as Encounter: Beyond the Teaching Imperative* (Lanham, MD: Rowman & Littlefield) 2022.

Sydney food courts in which I have eaten dozens of quick and fragrant bowls of broth, beef, and bok choi. As if I could, if I ate fast enough and focused hard enough on the cheap chopsticks, the black bowl, the cheap white spoon with a sharp edge, be not here in this bright, loud, subterranean space, gripping the edges of a hard plastic tray. Be elsewhere.

But I think, despite the stallholder's assurance, that the broth was made with soy sauce. At the time of this encounter, I had recently discovered that I am intolerant to gluten.[14] My body fights hard against what I believe it understands as a toxin, as food-that-lies, food that promises to soothe, to nourish, and instead it causes pain. Almost immediately after I finish the noodles I leave the food court in a fog. I'm so tired. I buy chocolate. I see if sugar will lift me out of the haze, clarify my thoughts, and feed the new need for clarity that is layered over the original need for comfort. I have to get myself together because I'm on another panel in half an hour. I decide to go to the scheduled room early, hope that it's empty, and hope I can force my fragmented self back together with at least a semblance of coherence through the gluten-induced brain fog and the fatigue and the many layers of discontent and discomfort that led me to the noodles.

The noodles were my third mistake. Thinking about my experience at the conference panel that preceded (precipitated) the noodles brings to mind the title of a subreddit forum: *Thanks, I hate it*. The memories of the panel are still too big, too bright; to think about it directly is like staring at the sun. My mind skitters, catching moments, faces, folded arms, and fixed smiles, in an incoherent and asynchronous strobe of recollection. Thinking about the hours I spent in that room feels like the quiet scratching of my right thumbnail against my left wrist, at the tender skin above my watch strap in the softness beside the tendon. An old trick learned in quiet offices where "sharing" doesn't mean what I think it means, where it's not an exchange, founded in reciprocity and generosity, but a process of extraction, even emesis. And in pubs and at dinner tables where a reciprocal and generous connection is assumed but always haunted by the terror of (bringing/sharing/being) too much or not-enough. The quiet scratching of my right thumbnail against my

---

[14] Other intolerances were later revealed: dairy, caffeine, nightshades, soy, and refined sugar. I have found a diet that mostly suits me after several years of painful trial and error, strict exclusions and careful monitoring of intake and reactions. As someone with a long history of disordered eating, this was challenging.

left wrist is the feeling of staying in place when a place and the feeling it engenders are not staying in me, can't be contained in me, and want to spill out and over and I should have left.

That was the second mistake. I should have left. Instead, I worked at staying, and I shouldn't have done that because it was too much for me. The professional obedience that kept me in that seat, the respect for my colleagues which meant I couldn't disrupt or disavow the discussion that was causing me such anguish—I had no place to put that. "I'm afraid," I said. "Every fiber of my being is uncomfortable," I said. I laughed, at first, but then I folded further and further in on myself until I wanted to be gone, entirely gone. I should have left.

I didn't leave. I stayed, because I wanted it to nourish me. I wanted the encounter to stop hurting and do good for me, for everyone in the room, and the needs and desires that brought them to this Lord of the Flies hotel room on a rainy Saturday in March. I signed up because I thought it would do good. Like the noodles, it was supposed to softly, warmly, fill me, but instead I fought it and it defeated me, poisoned me. I stayed, in this galaxy of emptiness, silent, quietly scratching, and so sad. I should have left.

So there was a prior mistake and it's that mistake I think that had me sitting in a badly made airplane seat after fifteen hours of flying, vomiting the first draft of this text into the Notes app on my iPad. I thought I could give of myself safely. I feel somehow that I didn't give enough of myself at this conference, but it was also too much. I flew home two days later and by then had sufficient distance from the immediacy of the wounding to at least recognize how and why I was hurt in the interaction, the sense of having been opened and shown—known—as fragile was beginning to scab over, and I was recovering. I made a mistake: there is a difference, it turns out, between intellectualizing through writing of a vulnerable self and enacting that vulnerability.

I find this profoundly disconcerting, for I don't know where it leaves me. I have always thought myself free in my writing; I delight in language, in playing with how words feel and taste in my mouth, and how they can in combination be transformed to create something unexpected, sometimes unexpectedly joyful, and always a part of me. I give of myself in my writing, and it is an effort, and a transformative reckoning with my own process of encountering the world. Hence, vulnerability. I wrote, in preparation for these discussions, of vulnerability. I was, as I said to others, "excited and somewhat trepidatious" to see where these discussions led.

I was trepidatious, but not afraid. I was not afraid that I would end up feeling/knowing my own vulnerability in a way for which I was entirely unprepared. I was not afraid that I would end up feeling bloodied and confused, an absent presence in discussions about my own professional (always personal) life. I was not afraid that I would be left concussed and empty, empty enough to take a chance on a bowl of food court noodles that would fight me like this experience fought me and leave me even more hollow, alone. I was not afraid.

But my stomach churned even as I tried to apprehend and still and make sense of the kaleidoscopic dazzle of snatched moments of memory. And now, I am afraid. I am afraid that I have uncovered some previously unsuspected layer of tenderness that was protected beneath that which is/was safe to explore. I suspect now that writing is and always has been a simple expression of the skin I am in; this experience tattooed me, exposed me, and I am undone. Now, I am afraid.

PART 3: UNBECOMING

From a place of distance, perhaps I can write myself whole again, heal again. Perhaps I can unbecome the wounded and fearful girl who knows nothing but her own vulnerability, her own pain. From this place of distance, I can reflect on those experiences, reflect on what—if anything—I know now about vulnerability, and fear, and courage. The first time I had a breakdown, I spent hours phoning the landline in my mother's house when I knew she was at work, because the image of the green plastic wall-mounted telephone filling her kitchen with sound soothed me, transported me back to that place of safety, where I could cede responsibility for my well-being to someone else, someone better qualified than I, it seemed, to take care of my needs. I wore black, and maintained a list in my head of "safe foods." The second time I had a breakdown, I had my hair cut to an inch all over and ran and swam and trained at the dojo three times a week, wearing the bruises on my thin forearms like armor. Vulnerability, and fear, and courage look different on me now.

Paulo Ravecca uses the motif of "epistemological temperature"[15] to guide his reader through the interwoven accounts of his life experience

---

[15] Paulo Ravecca, *The Politics of Political Science: Re-Writing Latin American Experiences* (London: Routledge) 2019, p.211.

and his engagement with the politics of political science: some chapters are "cold," he explains, maintaining the fiction of objectivity and distance, detachment and disengaged evaluation of the "facts" at hand, while others are "hot," reckoning with anger, fear, and outrage, and recognizing the emotionality of those encounters, whether with literature or personal pain. Mine perhaps is a motif of epistemological density, the concertina effect of integration and dis-integration of my self and the concomitant impact on my ability to be seen in, and sustained by, the relational connections not only that hold me in place but hold me together. Perhaps density is not quite the right word.

I have a lecture in my repertoire on ethics and Science Fiction, despite being an "expert" on neither.[16] I give this lecture each semester, in my current position, to students enrolled in the course on the politics of popular culture. I am very honest with them that I am neither ethicist, nor philosopher, nor SciFi fan. I encourage them to question my expertise, because I know that they won't. This is a lecture that invites discussion, shares ideas, and explores alternatives, building on the premise that, as a form of speculative fiction,[17] SciFi is uniquely placed to facilitate, even encourage, reflection on how we might live good lives. This is because, as Paul Kirby explains,

> [i]n attending to . . . the fragmented specimens of dreamworlds as much as formulaic correspondences, we may better parse the codes of culture beyond analogical appropriation: the strange and spectral demarcation of future worlds that are somehow already here, augmentations and mutilations, portending and refusing in equal measure, always ultimately in excess of analogy and political certainty, and sometimes signifying nothing of import at all.[18]

In the borderland between the fictive and the real is a place from which we can imagine "future worlds that are somehow already here"; in the lecture, I argue that SciFi thus offers a space to think about ethical obligation and political community beyond our current limited

---

[16] The lecture is based in part on an article that I published on the same topic, but it is particularly the lecture I am reflecting on here. If you are interested, the article is: William Clapton and Laura J. Shepherd, "*Ethics Ex Machina*: Popular Culture and the Plural Futures of Politics," *Australian Journal of Political Science*, 2019, 54(4): 531–542.

[17] Paul Kirby, "Political Speech in Fantastical Worlds." *International Studies Review*, 2017, 19(4): 573–596, p.575 and throughout.

[18] Kirby, "Political Speech in Fantastical Worlds," pp.591–592.

imagining, and, in part, it does so by presenting accounts of how we might interact in future worlds with those we recognize and categorize as "non-human."

The first time I gave this lecture, it was a guest appearance in a course on politics and popular culture that a colleague was convening. It was the third or fourth lecture I had given to this particular group of students, and I was tentatively establishing something of a friendship with the convenor; we were moving cautiously into a closer connection, and I was disclosing pains of the body that interfered with my lecturing (more so in those days, I suffered chronic migraines and more than once lectured or attended meetings zoned out on triptans and wearing sunglasses) and intellectual discomforts that interfered with my teaching in a different way. As we walked back to our office building that day, I was reflecting on whether the content was too dense, wondering aloud whether I had moved through the material too rapidly, expecting too much, or not giving enough. No doubt I was expecting reassurance. But my colleague gently, generously, refused; she asked instead what students might make of the presentation and exploration of these issues of relationality, connectivity, and ethical obligation to non-human others through the lens of SciFi when there was such a rich tradition of thinking in this way in Indigenous philosophy.

This was not the response I anticipated. My colleague's words made my throat constrict and my skin prickle. I was ashamed. I reflected on the lecture I had just given and wished desperately that I could unteach that class, unspeak those words, and cover the nakedness of my ignorance with pages and words and better thoughts. I probably didn't (want to) admit this at the time. I was not brave, in my not-knowing, at that moment. I did not have courage. I was undone.[19]

This lecture, which I have revised, and delivered many times since, still haunts me. I actually hate it now. I hate how it reminds me of my shortcomings, my foolishness, and my fallibility. Even as I make the point, now, that these musings on connectivity and relationality that have begun to seep into Western philosophy have a much longer history and heritage in a literature that is widely and wildly ignored by most of

---

[19] Ironically, given that there is a discussion in this lecture about being "undone in the face of the other"; see: Judith Butler, *Precarious Life: The Powers of Mourning and Violence* (London, Verso) 2006.

the academy,[20] it is infused with shame and a choking sense of failure. It takes a different kind of courage to stand in front of new students each year and admit my failings. There I can stand, though, because in the performance of admission, I can sometimes find my way to the students and meet them in a shared space of unknowing, of not yet knowing. I carry that brief conversation with my colleague in my teaching heart, although its sharp edges draw blood if I am careless with the memory. It gives me courage, because it connects me with her, and the students, and it reminds me that I am held in these relations of accountability and it reminds me that I am held.

I come back again and again to holding and being held, to vulnerability in the pedagogical encounter and the question of to whom I am accountable, to whom I owe obligation in the classroom. I imagine hot sand or damp earth beneath my feet when I am distracted from formatting PowerPoint slides; I watch the light on leaves and silver bark and as the sun falls I cherish birdsong in the half-light. As much as literature, these connections are in my pedagogy, in my heart.

At a symposium held in Sydney in 2019, Michelle Lee Brown taught me the concept of "more-than-human kin," as we all reflected together on place and peace and relationships and learning. I spent time at that event thinking about how my encounters with the more-than-human have nourished me. The relationships, the connections, that are in my bones, have been shaped by soul. There are places of my past that hold me and heal me—fen soil, smooth pebble coastline, the gentle green smell of English summer grass—and the same is true of the land that I live on presently, the soft sandstone and shorelines of my world now. I have walked to the ocean and stood with my feet in the cool salt water and wept tears of pure relief. I have learned I have more to learn about how I am in and how I understand and encounter the world.[21]

---

[20] I'd like you to imagine that I am narrowing my eyes and pursing my lips in disapproval in the general direction of Judith Butler as you read this, for her recent essay in *Time* magazine. Judith Butler, "Creating an Inhabitable World for Humans Means Dismantling Rigid Forms of Individuality," *TIME*, April 21, 2021. Online, at https://time.com/5953396/judith-butler-safe-world-individuality/.

[21] For two beautiful reflections on place, relationality, and knowing, see: Bawaka Country, Sarah Wright, Sandie Suchet-Pearson, Kate Lloyd, Laklak Burarrwanga, Ritjilili Ganambarr, Merrkiyawuy Ganambarr-Stubbs, Banbapuy Ganambarr, Djawundil Maymuru, and Jill Sweeney, "Co-becoming Bawaka: Towards a Relational Understanding of Place/Space," *Progress in Human Geography*, 2016, 40(4): 455–475; and Lauren Tynan, "What is Relationality? Indigenous Knowledges, Practices and Responsibilities with Kin," *Cultural Geographies*, 2021, 28(4): 597–610.

Rock Formation. Photo by author.

When organizing the symposium, my dear co-host (friend, co-conspirator) and I asked a representative from the local Aboriginal land council if they would welcome our guests to Gadigal country, the stolen land on which the symposium was held. He came and invoked the spirits of his ancestors, the elders of the Gadigal people, to walk with us as we convened. I heard this generosity, and I appreciated it, but I didn't fully absorb it, didn't really feel it, until we broke for lunch on the following day. I walked out into the sun, to feel and heal, and I saw a colleague passing by. She had actually registered for the symposium but had not been able to attend. She told me how sorry she was, and how hopeless she felt. How overwhelmed she was by her life at the moment, how out of control. She shared it with me, and she apologized. I asked if she was hungry, and I was able to lead her back inside, to encourage her to take a plate of food to sustain her for the rest of the day. She told me that she had just come from an appointment across town, how she was heading for her office to finish a grant application, and how worried she was about seeming incompetent, and she apologized. I hugged her, and fed her, and I heard her apology but affirmed her energy and efforts. I told her that this event reminded me that we should spend more time feeding, and hugging, and affirming people. I told her about the welcome we had been extended, and how we had been gifted the company of Gadigal ancestors, walking with us. I believe that those ancestors brought her into my path that sunny afternoon, so I could hug her, and feed her, and assure her that she is held in relations that will sustain her. I am her kin, and she is mine.

In the months since, I have continued to read a little on "connectivity thinking,"[22] which is grounded in ecology, to understand social ontology, and relationality, and little differently. In some Indigenous philosophy—which theorizes politics from the perspective of the entire physical and spiritual universe, rather than from the perspective of the human or the social—"works of social relations are intrinsic to one's sense of self and composite identities, rather than extrinsic (as in an individualistic notion of the person)."[23] I have begun to develop a wider understanding of the relations that hold me in place and that hold me. I have begun to develop a deeper and more integrated sense of what nourishes and sustains me, and how these people, places, and things connect me with me and with different ways of being and knowing. I have begun to learn, rather than to try, or try to teach, which I feel takes courage of a different order. "I do not understand human existence, and the struggle needed to improve it, apart from hope and dream."[24] I do not understand how to unbecome, how to live undone, but to find a place to stand, a place to stay, to act with intent and calm integrity, is a guide and an aspiration.

Don Hamachek suggests that being an "effective teacher" is a function of self-knowledge: "Consciously, we teach what we know; unconsciously, we teach who we are"[25] (Hamachek 1999, p. 209). I wonder whether consciously, I teach who I am, and unconsciously, I teach who I wish I could be. I am increasingly uncertain that I know anything such that I could teach it, or perhaps it is more that I don't know how to teach the things that I think I know. I suspect it is because *consciously* I teach who I am that it makes me feel so exposed; I wonder if it is working the grain of that vulnerability that enables some fleeting connections

---

[22] Deborah Bird Rose, "Connectivity Thinking, Animism, and the Pursuit of Liveliness," *Educational Theory*, 2017, 67(4): 491–508.

[23] Sylvie Poirier, quoted in Sylvie Poirier, "Reflections on Indigenous Cosmopolitics—Poetics," *Anthropologica*, 2008, 50(1): 75–85, p.78. See also: Deborah Bird Rose, "Cosmopolitics: The Kiss of Life," *New Formations*, 2012, 76: 101–113.

[24] Freire, *Pedagogy of Hope*, p.2.

[25] Don Hamachek, "Effective Teachers: What They Do, How They Do It, and the Importance of Self-Knowledge," 189–224 in Richard P. Lipka and Thomas M. Brinthaupt, eds, *The Role of Self in Teacher Development* (Albany, NY: State University of New York Press) 1999, p.209.

with students, when (if) such a thing is possible. For sure, I have little expertise to claim, beyond surviving vulnerability in the academy, being here, and showing up. Perhaps that is the (tentative, fragmented, and formation-in-process) foundation of my courage.

Chapter 3

Encounter

I wrote this chapter in 2016 having recently returned to my normal duties, after a nourishing, nurturing, magnificent six-month sabbatical.[1] *I struggled to carve out the time—in between meetings with colleagues, responding to the demands of senior management, and dealing with complaints from students, in my capacity as Deputy Head of School—to re-engage with these ideas, which traveled with me from Sydney to London and back again, quietly wondering when their time would come. This is part of the story: the self I account for in the pages that follow is in tension with the self who could not find time to make this account. And this is part of the context: where are the silences in the selves we admit to, and why do we validate some selves and not others?*

Research is demanding. It is time-consuming, painstaking, fear-inducing, sometimes tedious, and always intense. I began thinking about the themes of this chapter as I brought to conclusion a major research project, a project that demanded a lot of me as both a scholar and a person. It was the first major funded project I had undertaken since my doctoral research, and the first of my research ventures to involve "field research" (more on that below). I experienced a number of challenges in its execution, experiences which led me to reflect on the practice

[1] This is a lightly edited version of an essay previously published as: Laura J. Shepherd, "Research as Gendered Intervention: Feminist Research Ethics and the Self in the Research Encounter," *Crítica Contemporánea: Revista de Teoría Política*, 2016, p.6.

of research as a sequence or collection of performative acts and the imbrication of my self (my inescapably gendered self) in my research practice. In the process of deliberating, or reflecting upon, the ways in which an "I"—as a researcher, as an academic, and as a feminist—have been constituted through my research practices, I began to consider also the ways in which this "I" is disciplined: what are the dimensions of silence around the constitution of my self and how do these silences reveal the significance of making such reflective accounts, within a feminist research ethic? I am guided by Naeem Inayatullah's refusal to "ontologize" myself (my "I" self); I do not make these claims on behalf of an essential, stable "I," nor do I think that "I" am the most interesting feature of the social world that I both encounter an inhabit. But I do think that "exposure and disclosure of the self/selves, rather than locating some idiosyncratic 'n of 1' or some *sui generis* entity, instead uncovers events, histories, cultures, and worlds."[2] The world I uncover here are the worlds of the academy in late modernity, but I will abandon this thought for the moment and begin instead by telling a story or two.

The first of these stories begins, sort of, with my move from the United Kingdom to Australia, and then, within a year or two of that happening, with the election of Australia to a two-year term of office on the UN Security Council. I have worked with UN documents, particularly Security Council resolutions, often throughout my career; I find them endlessly fascinating. I love the form and cadence of the resolutions, the recitation of heritage and dues in the Preamble, and the textured layers of meaning in the operative paragraphs made all the richer by knowing that every single word in every single resolution is negotiated and agreed upon by the present members of the Council. I love that sometimes this negotiation happens at speed, and really interesting bits of language sneak through. I love that academics fight constantly about the status of SC resolutions in international law; there's general agreement that resolutions of the Council acting under Chapter VII of the UN Charter are binding but we continue to debate whether resolutions are generally binding on member states or simply impose specific obligations upon those states on a case-by-case basis. The question of legal standing, and the argumentation presented by both sides, tends to

---

[2] Naeem Inayatullah, "Falling and Flying: An Introduction," 1–12 in Naeem Inayatullah, ed., *Autobiographical International Relations: I, IR* (London and New York: Routledge) 2011, p.8.

hinge on language, which is perhaps why I find the resolutions and the field of debates so engaging.

I love Security Council resolutions and much of my research involves engaging with such documents, particularly those produced under the auspices of the Women, Peace and Security agenda. I am also fascinated by the politics of the Council, by the significance of the five permanent members to the institutional politics of the UN more broadly and by the rotation of the ten elected members and related shifts in priority and focus of the Council from month to month as the presidency too rotates among the membership. With Australia occupying one of the E-10 seats for two years, my new Australian colleagues and I made many efforts to engage the government and advocate for a strong and consistent commitment to championing the Women, Peace and Security agenda at the UN for the duration of the term of office. I wrote letters (never more than a page), I made phone calls (sometimes, but not often, to the right people at the right time), and I attended a large number of consultations with the Department of Foreign Affairs and Trade (DFAT) throughout the two years.

I would get up in the morning, early, to catch a flight down to Canberra for these consultations. I would travel to the airport in a taxi, and I would cross the Sydney Harbour Bridge feeling somewhat smugly accomplished at having been invited to participate in the day's meetings, trying to ignore the gritty-eyed tiredness and generalized sense of imposture. I would make my way to the DFAT building and wait in the foyer to be escorted through to the meeting room; I would shake hands with the other participants and respond, when asked my name, "I'm Laura Shepherd. I'm an academic," by way of explanation for my presence. I said it all in one breath, as though the second naming was as essential as the first. I invoked the academy as a protection, as a justification, to benefit from its associations. "I'm an academic," I said. I did not say: "I'm an expert"; "I'm a thinker of profound and important thoughts"; "I belong." These things I left unsaid, I let my simple introduction do the work for me: "I'm an academic." I cloaked myself in these words, but they failed to shield me from feeling like I was somehow out of place, like I did not belong. I would leave these consultations charged with guilt. I had not contributed enough, I told myself. I had not served the house of power with sufficient diligence. I was so enraptured, seduced anew each time I received an invitation to a consultation, I didn't stop to think for very long about what earthly use a discourse theorist might be in a policy discussion. But each time, I dismissed immediately the notion of declining. "I would be delighted to attend . . ." I wrote. "Thank you for your kind invitation . . ." I responded. "Of course I would be happy to join you to discuss . . ." Of course. I'm an academic.

And now my second story: I like words. I find the production of meaning fascinating, and teasing out the practices of meaning-production is deeply gratifying. I am wholly comfortable working with documents, statements, resolutions, and other kinds of textual artifacts. And yet, for this most recent research project, I decided to undertake interviews. I'm still not entirely sure where this impulse came from. When I wrote up the application for funding for this project, back in 2012, I used lots of words I had left in the dark recesses of my brain to gather dust since the conclusion of my Masters in Social Science Research Methods. "Sample," "snowball," "semi-structured": they were unfamiliar and strange yet felt seductive in their scientific status (and their sibilance). Writing this account of my research felt like the performance of "proper" social scientist, affirmed by the award of a grant from the Australian Research Council to undertake this research, to do this "fieldwork."

Except I didn't go to "the field," of course, whatever that might mean; Oliver Richmond, Stefanie Kappler, and Annika Björkdahl have written beautifully about the compromised conceptual status of "the field" in peace research, arguing that it "carries colonial baggage in terms of denoting 'backwardness' and conflictual practices, as well as legitimizing the need for intervention by peacebuilding, statebuilding and development actors."[3] I concur with their reading of "the field" as frequently represented in scholarship on peacebuilding and development, but mine was a different field. I didn't go to their field. I went to New York, in the summer of 2013 and then again in 2014. I rattled around the city trying to keep cool in the slick, sweaty heat, with Ani DiFranco lyrics about the East River and the F train in my head; I winced at people drinking iced black coffee, which I maintain is an abomination, and my child developed a taste for chocolate frozen yogurt. We explored Central Park on the weekend, danced under the sprinklers in the play park, and I watched my child play with joy and

---

[3] Annika, Björkdahl, Oliver Richmond and Stefanie Kappler, "The Field in the Age of Intervention: Power, Legitimacy, Authority vs the 'Local'," *Millennium: Journal of International Studies*, 2015, 44(1): 23–44, p.25.

thought about my next interview, or my last interview, or how good it felt to have told people, "Yeah, we're going to New York in the summer, I'm doing some work on peacebuilding at the UN." It made me feel like a proper researcher, whereas working with documents (or, worse still, with television shows, of which I have also been guilty) has always made me feel somehow *less than* proper.

"I'm doing fieldwork," I would tell myself, as I handed over my passport to the security staff at the East 46th Street gate, receiving in return a grainy and unflattering temporary ID allowing me access to UN HQ. "I'm doing fieldwork," I thought, as I took a screenshot of my iPad connecting to the wifi network and shared it on Facebook. "I'm doing fieldwork," I reminded myself, as I eventually remembered to switch on my little hand-held audio recorder and steer the conversation with those kind enough to meet with me around to peacebuilding, and away from restaurant recommendations and the delights of the New York Hall of Science for a tech-obsessed five-year-old. "I'm doing fieldwork." "I'm an academic."

So those are two little vignettes that sit with me, weigh on me, and have inspired me to think about what those statements mean, as I have struggled to make sense of these, and other research encounters: "I'm an academic," "I'm doing fieldwork." What does it mean to make those claims? Who is this person, this self of whom I am, in Judith Butler's terms, attempting to give an account? When I embark with a new research student upon a new supervisory journey, I talk to them about research. One of my favorite aphorisms to share is the etymology of the word "research." It comes from Old French, *re-*, meaning "with intensity or force" and *cerchier*, meaning "to search." So "research" means to search with intensity, to search closely, to seek. I talk then with my new students about what it is they are seeking, what they hope that their journey will show them, what is it that ultimately they think they might find. I have found that, for me, the research process is a process of seeking. I have sought documents that codify slippery and unstable meanings momentarily, the logics of which produce an architecture that is unique to its time but also timeless in its form and structure. I have sought "research participants" to talk to about stuff, to whom I most singularly fail to explain eloquently what it is that I seek, though I expect them to join me in my investigation. I have sought permission from the Human Research Ethics Approval Panel to talk to those same research participants, and fumed at what I perceived to be nonsensical modifications demanded to enable my research to be deemed "ethical," whatever that means. I have sought answers, to research questions that I determined prior, as if we can ever really know what our question is before we begin our research journey with an open heart and a curious mind. And I have sought validation. "I'm doing fieldwork," because anyone who can read can tell you what a Security Council resolution says, so where is the value in that? "I'm an academic," because what I really mean to say is, "I'm an expert, I belong here. Accept this. Accept me."

So we seek, when we research, when we *re-cerchier*, and also, we find. I have found my self—or, more accurately, my selves—as I have practiced my research and as I have encountered my research worlds. I am produced as I research. Intuitively this is true: I am produced as a scholar worthy of note (worthy of publication or promotion) as I practice my research, and it secures me competitively allocated external funding or plaudits from peers. I reproduce this when I write the next funding application, or application for promotion, or proposal for a book or a Special Issue of a journal, and as I reproduce this identity so the "I" who makes these claims is constituted. But there are interesting silences in the accounts of myself that I give in these formal domains. I do not speak of my insecurities, my sense of imposture, my fear that I—not my work, but *I*—am not "proper" in the eyes of my discipline. These echoing silences prompt reflection: who is this "I," and who is she not? Of what "I" are these particular practices performative? What is my responsibility to this "I," when I am driven half-mad by a desire to play hooky and keep my child out of school for the day, to bundle us into the car and drive to the ocean and join hands floating head back in the murky blue water looking up at the brilliant blue sky, so we can feel but not see each others' smiles, feel only that and nothing else?

Research may be a quest, but it is also productive, and not in the ways caught in the limited imagination of the neoliberal university. Research produces us, our selves as researchers, just as the practices of research we perform "enact our worlds," to paraphrase Claudia Aradau and Jef Huysmans.[4] I have been deeply inspired by Aradau and Huysman's brilliant essay on the politics of methodology, which also has as

---

[4] Claudia Aradau, and Jef Huysmans, "Critical Methods in International Relations: The Politics of Techniques, Devices and Acts," *European Journal of International Relations*, 2014, 20(3): 596–619.

its focus the productivity of research. As they say, methods need to be understood as performative rather than representational. They are not simply techniques of extracting information from reality and aligning it with—or against—bodies of knowledge. Methods are instead within worlds and partake in their shaping. Performative methods are practices through which "truthful" worlds are enacted, both in the sense of being acted upon and coming into being.[5]

To their insightful exposition, I would suggest that we, as researchers (and mothers, co-workers, life partners, voracious readers, and bakers of delicious treats) are of these worlds, we come into being through our research practices at the same time as we enact them.

This has felt more true for me in this recent research than in other projects I have undertaken, and this is not a controversial intellectual step to take, I think. As Aradau and Huysmans show, reconfiguring the terrain of discussion over methods in International Relations (IR) foregrounds the productive power of methods as acts that bring into being certain objects, and subjects, and the relations between them while disrupting other. Reading this insight through a decade or more steeped in the theorization of identity as performance raises the question of where the "self" is located in Aradau and Huysman's analysis and how the self is enacted. I am responding to the deliberation in *Critical Security Methods: New Frameworks for Analysis*, where the editors encourage us as readers to ask "what method does as a practice,"[6] trying to extend their critical engagement with the politics of method to explore the performative constitution of the self through research. Put simply, I theorize that Aradua and Huysmans are on to something: methods enact the world. But research—including but not limited to methods—also enacts the self, the "I" who claims: "I'm doing fieldwork, I'm an academic."

And this is, of course, a fundamentally gendered process. Gender, as Cynthia Enloe notably remarked, makes the world go round:[7] it structures how we think about, and act in, the world, and orders the relationship between bodies and behaviors. This is as true for the researcher as

---

[5] Aradau and Huysmans, "Critical Methods in International Relations," p.598.
[6] Claudia Aradau, Jef Huysmans, Andrew Neal and Nadine Voelkner, "Introducing Critical Security Methods," 1–22 in Claudia Aradau, Jef Huysmans, Andrew Neal and Nadine Voelkner, eds, *Critical Security Methods: New Frameworks for Analysis* (London and New York, NY: Routledge) 2015, p.6.
[7] Cynthia Enloe, *Bananas, Beaches and Bases: Making Feminist Sense of International Politics*, rev. edn. (Berkeley, CA: University of California Press) 2000, p.1 and throughout.

it is for the politician, the firefighter, and the artist. We cannot escape being read through the lens of our gender presentation, and our gendered identities are produced through our research practices just as they are produced through any other of the social practices in which we engage. We cannot escape the logics of research as a gendered intervention.

As I mused on the question of how my self and my research are co-constituted, I pondered also the question of what makes this research feminist. Is it enough that I espouse, overtly and publicly, a feminist politics? Is it enough that I am attentive to the dynamics of gendered power? That I am always looking to understand better how gendered power operates in any given discursive terrain, including the terrains in/through which I am produced as a subject: the academy, the research encounter, the journal article, the meandering discussions over dinner with friends? In my search for an answer to the question of what is feminist about feminist research, I found no more eloquent account than that provided by Sharlene Nagy Hesse-Biber. She explains:

> To engage in feminist theory and praxis means to challenge knowledge that excludes, while seeming to include . . . Feminists ask "new" questions that place women's lives and those of "other" marginalized groups at the center of social inquiry. Feminist research disrupts traditional ways of knowing to create rich new meanings, a process that Trinh (1991) terms becoming "both/and"—insider and outsider—taking on a multitude of different standpoints and negotiating these identities simultaneously.[8]

We feminists challenge, in our research practices, we disrupt and we look opposite, beyond, and sideways at the conventional sites of inquiry. We unsettle that which is frequently taken for granted, including the very categories we use to think with, the identities we perform, and those structures of comfortable, comforting, privilege and power we enjoy.

I can bear being disruptive. Even the writing of this account is a form of disruption, but it is a disruption (of scholarly conventions and expectations) performed by a self to whom certain privilege has accrued. I can choose to spend my time writing this account, to invest effort

---

[8] Sharlene Nagy Hesse-Biber, "Feminist Research: Exploring, Interrogating, and Transforming the Interconnections of Epistemology, Methodology, and Method," 2–26 in Sharlene Nagy Hesse-Biber, ed., *Handbook of Feminist Research: Theory and Praxis* (London: SAGE) 2012, p.3.

and energy in these reflections and revelations, and not fear reprisal or reprimand for having expended my resources in this way, for I have reached a stage in my career at which, especially when combined with the luxury of employment security, I am driven not by institutional imperatives but by my own. There are other fears, of course, touched upon in previous chapters: as Inayatullah admits, "we fear our revelations will mark us for having indulged in navel-gazing and for having showcased our vanity,"[9] but these are fears of a different order that do not touch me at the precise moment that I sit down to consider really what it means to me to disrupt, to be both inside and outside, to practice feminist research.

When turning over the question in my mind, of how a feminist self is constituted through feminist research, rather than simply building on my account of feminist research to argue that the converse logic holds (if feminist research pays attention to the "concept, nature, and practice of gender," per Zalewski's formulation,[10] then research that pays attention to the "concept, nature, and practice of gender" is done by feminists, QED), I arrive at the question of science. I am reminded of "the science question" in the design of each research project I propose, as I am so easily seduced by the scientism of the social research methods I promise to "employ" (as though methods are tools that can be applied to a willing world, to extract with ease the knowledge that lies undisturbed within, waiting only for the right question to be asked in order that this knowledge might spring forth and bathe the research in the soft glow of enlightenment). Feminist research attends to the gendered dynamics of power that have historically excluded women from the subject position of "authentic knower" or "figure of authority" yet recognizes that in the practices of feminist research stow away the privilege of authority and authenticity that we critique.

This point of argumentation is of course indebted to Sandra Harding, and her posing of *The Science Question in Feminism*: "Is it possible," she asks, "to use for emancipatory ends sciences that are apparently so intimately involved in Western, bourgeois, and masculine projects?"[11] In the practice of using such sciences, I would venture, I am implicated

---

[9] Inayatullah, "Falling and Flying," pp.7–8.
[10] Marysia Zalewski, "Well, What is the Feminist Perspective on Bosnia?," *International Affairs*, 1995, 71(2): 339–356, p.339.
[11] Sandra Harding, *The Science Question in Feminism* (Ithaca, NJ: Cornell University Press) 1986, p.9.

as a feminist researcher in the "Western, bourgeois, and masculine projects" and I benefit from the authority that such an association brings. By simple virtue of my association with the academy, even as I present my unruly, poststructural, adventures in language for evaluation, I am performed as an authoritative figure, if not a figure of authority. "I'm an academic." Feminist research is intensely attuned to power and is yet complicit in its exercise when I—as a feminist researcher—claim its benefit. The feminist self performed in this exercise, then, is recognizable as Janet Halley's "governance feminist"; discomfittingly, I invoke the power of science in order to "walk the halls" of political power.[12] I am embarrassed to admit this, and I wonder what it means for my feminism and my research.

So the feminist self-produced through my research is curious, yes, but also conflicted, and compromised. I reflect on this, as I move in and through the spaces of my research. I think about what to wear to walk those halls of power, to meet with the UN staff who are generously giving of their time, and I am immediately furious with myself for caring even a little, as though my feminism should elevate me above such base concerns. I examine my decisions (sartorial and otherwise) unflinchingly: have you noticed that we are rarely as kind to ourselves as we can be to others? And I wonder: what does this mean for me, as a feminist, as a researcher, as a being in the world? Can I separate my feminist self from my researcher self, from all my other selves? Am I a feminist? Am I an academic? My self is inextricably bound up in my research, I feel.

I feel. My back aches, up into my right shoulder, because I wore heels yesterday, unusually for me, and I do not sit comfortably at my desk. My body tells a story of my professional life and my manifest inability to practice constructive levels of self-care; I grind my teeth, I suffer from migraine, I have perpetual tension in my jaw and shoulders, and I feel pain like guilt that I am failing myself so I can succeed for others. My self-hood is woven through my research practices, as I account for the choices that I make and explain how and why I came to the decisions that I did during the conduct of research. I am implicated in, and produced through, my research practices. According to Kim England, "part of the feminist project has been to dismantle the smokescreen surrounding the canons of neopositivist research—impartiality and

---

[12] Janet Halley, *Split Decisions: How and Why to Take a Break from Feminism* (Princeton, NJ: Princeton University Press) 2006, p.21.

objectivist neutrality—which supposedly prevent the researcher from contaminating the data (and, presumably, vice versa)."[13] I am a contaminant. Am I a feminist? Am I an academic? The practice of research—the search—is the perfect performative moment of Foucault's power/knowledge nexus. Foucault theorized that power and knowledge are indivisible, two sides of the same coin: there can be no claim to know that is not simultaneously an expression of power, and every expression of power carries with it, overtly or covertly, a claim to know. Foucault even indicted academic researchers directly in the production of knowledge claims, when he proposed that "It is necessary to think of the political problems of intellectuals not in terms of 'science' and 'ideology' but in terms of 'truth' and 'power'."[14] Foucault implicates "science" as a regime of truth, an assemblage of statements that pre- and proscribe that which is thinkable in regard to a given issue. If the target of our investigation is knowledge itself, then we must recognize that the circumstances of knowledge production—again, to quote Foucault, "the systems of power that produce and sustain it, and [the] effects of power which it induces and which extend it"[15]—operate according to a logic of science. The subject, produced through research, then—even in the face of avowedly post- or anti-positivist declarations to the contrary—is the subject of science, the scientist.

In this context, the work of Patrick Jackson appeals to me in its incisive critique of the disciplinary function of "science" in IR. As Jackson says, "in IR—the context in which I research, and am therefore (re) produced—'science' remains a notion to conjure with . . . and a powerful resource it is too: charging that a piece of work is not 'scientific' carries immensely negative connotations."[16] Even as a feminist, even as I look opposite, beyond, and sideways at the conventional sites of inquiry, I perform my research credentials in accordance with the logic of science because this is the connotation of the academy that I claim.

---

[13] Kim V. L. England, "Getting Personal: Reflexivity, Positionality, and Feminist Research," *The Professional Geographer*, 1994, 46(1): 80–89, p.81.

[14] Michel Foucault, *Power: Essential Works of Foucault 1954–1984, vol 3*, ed. James D. Faubion, trans. Robert Hurley and others (London: Penguin Book) [1994] 2000, p.132.

[15] Foucault, *Power: Essential Works of Foucault 1954–1984*.

[16] Patrick Thaddeus Jackson, *The Conduct of Inquiry in International Relations: Philosophy of Science and Its Implications for the Study of World Politics* (London and New York, NY: Routledge) 2001, p.9.

When I make that claim, I'm not a writer, or a theorist, or even a feminist: I'm an academic.

So I travel to meetings in Canberra alone, and sit alongside (but not with, not really, not *with*) the many others in the room and I think my interior thoughts and I stay, quiet, and watchful. I sit in airless, over-conditioned meeting rooms in New York and fumble with my papers and wait for the hot flash of shame to pass when I am asked for a business card and I cannot readily provide one. I squirm, uncomfortable in the entirely not ergonomic desk chair in my office, and I cross the floor to retrieve a book to flick through, as though the words of other people will save me when the opposite is true: I will drown in them, in their words, and my own blank spaces, and the helpless teeth-grinding awfulness of having nothing new to say. I draft a tweet with a link to my latest article—can I find the right degree of self-deprecation, the appropriately humble yet accomplished tone?—before updating my university profile page lest anyone visit and be misled by the absence of this crucial detail about me. I am an academic. I am barely a feminist. I am not a mother, in these moments, nor a friend, a hopeless dancer, or a reckless driver. I am mostly alone.

How can this be otherwise, I wonder? How can I produce feminist research and be produced through this research in ways that feel true to me? How can I understand and make sense of the "I" that is produced through the research practices of a feminist self? The concept of positionality, to me, relates to the position of the researcher in relation to her research environment, and her position in the social world: it is a consciousness of self, but a self-assumed fully formed, a priori in the research process. Brooke Ackerly and Jacqui True propose that "[t]he researcher . . . needs to situate herself with respect to the ways in which being a researcher is itself a boundary that affects research."[17] I find this boundary to be porous: my positionings, which are inevitably multiple, both affect and effect what I bring to the research encounter. Crucially, I view positionality as inescapably relational: as we engage in research as a social encounter, those with whom we engage create positions for us in their cognitive frameworks, to make sense for themselves of who we are and what we bring. I am read through my gender, my race, my

---

[17] Brooke Ackerly and Jacqui True, "Reflexivity in Practice: Power and Ethics in Feminist Research on International Relations," *International Studies Review*, 2008, 10(4): 693–707, p.698.

nationality, and my class, and these readings position me differently in relation to my multiple others depending on the context in which I am encountered.

In the practice of my research, I make not only political claims about what exists in the world and how we can know it but also inescapably normative claims about the kind of world that I want to bring into being: in my case, one attuned to the operation of gendered power. How I constitute my research practice is, in the Butlerian sense, an account of my self: "And when we do act and speak, we not only disclose ourselves but act on the schemes of intelligibility that govern who will be a speaking being, subjecting them to rupture or revision, consolidating their norms, or contesting their hegemony."[18] And my self is constituted through these "schemes of intelligibility," always already in relation to the many others with whom I interact. Who counts in my research, which questions I ask, and the assumptions that I make about the validity and viability of different forms of knowledge are intrinsic elements of the research encounter. These elements are inevitably shaped by my subjectivity and emerge in and through my research practice; they are informed by and inform my engagement with people, books, fields, offices, social mediascapes, and seashores. I am grateful to all the people I have met in the course of my searches for what they have taught me. I carry them with me, and I am not alone after all. I am partly, but never wholly, the product of my searches, my seeking with intensity a better understanding of peace and security in a world that is always in process. I am a feminist. I am an academic.

It is in these affective connections that I find solace, even purpose; they enable me in ways that I cannot fully comprehend. Being a feminist, being an academic: these are relational identities for me, subject positions that cannot exist—not only philosophically but also in material, embodied sense—without others, but not others against whom to define myself but others with whom I can navigate these insecurities and explore the silences in the account that I give of my self. Carolyn Ellis asks, "Is ethnography only about the other? Isn't ethnography also relational, about the other and the 'I' of the researcher in interaction?

---

[18] Judith Butler, *Giving an Account of Oneself* (New York, NY: Fordham University Press) 2005, p.132.

Might the researcher also be a subject?"[19] to which I respond: I have made my self the subject of this exposition, but I am always a situated subject, and this brings not only comfort but also context. This auto-ethnography is always auto*ethno*graphy—of self, of people, of writing—and the relationality of the research practices through which I am produced is inextricably linked to its politics, and its purpose.

I opened by asking, where are the silences in the selves we admit to? I have laid bare dimensions of my self that were previously hidden. I have explored the qualities of the "I" constituted through research encounters, the nature of the relationship between feminist research ethic and feminist researcher, the seductive interpellative power of the subject of "expert" and the insecurities inherent in occupying that position. Prior to writing this chapter, these were not themes I had written on before and this was a voice I had silenced in my professional writings; there is a purpose, I believe, to speaking with this voice, a purpose beyond authenticity. Jackson, mentioned above, commented on his own stories: "I don't know what these stories mean; I don't know just what kind of work they do. I do know that they feel in some difficult-to-define sense like *authentic* expressions."[20] The account I am giving here—in this chapter, in this book—feels both like an authentic expression and a facsimile thereof, with that glittering seam of ambivalence running deep into the core of this offering. I am intrigued to explore further the question of "what kind of work" my account does.

I presented a draft of this chapter at the LSE Gender Institute, where I spent a very happy period as a Visiting Fellow during the 2016 sabbatical I mentioned above. I was terrified to give voice to these reflections, to perform this fragile, contingent, uncertain self, and to admit to the insecurities and failings that I acknowledge as part of the "I" that I am when I claim to be a feminist academic. I was anxious, in reading the chapter, not only because of the confessions previously unspoken and unacknowledged but also because I had not yet, at that stage, arrived at a reasonable response to the very legitimate question of why anyone in that audience should care about my rambling account of my fragmented selves. I knew then, as now, that I do not believe "that

---

[19] Carolyn Ellis, *The Ethnographic I: A Methodological Novel about Autoethnography* (Walnut Creek, CA: AltaMira Press) 2004, p.xix.

[20] Patrick Thaddeus Jackson, "Three Stories: A Way of Being in the World," 161–172 in Naeem Inayatullah, ed., *Autobiographical International Relations: I, IR* (London and New York: Routledge) 2011, p.172, emphasis in original.

'telling one's story' in a personally reflective way is enough to produce insightful scholarship or engender political transformation."[21] But I did not know when I began writing in this register how I could marshal this energy in a way that would feel both authentic, but also transformative. I am still unsure.

Much relies on the question of what exists to be transformed. Morgan Brigg and Roland Bleiker argue that part of the transformation that can be facilitated through the conduct of autoethnography is epistemological; the recognition that "insights through the self are always already formed in relationship with the world and others"[22] challenges the presumption that the "proper" academic is the lone star hero of her own social world and that "proper" academic knowledge is objective and—importantly—highly individualized. This epistemological transformation is significant, but I see the purpose of what I am presenting here slightly differently. The transformation I seek is both personal-political and disciplinary, or knowledge-political. IR as a discipline surely has difficulties with knowledge, and I have always been relatively ill-disciplined. There are professional risks, of course, in refusing to be bound by disciplines, and a degree of reckoning that is therefore required when thinking through the presentation of deliberation in this way, but there is also a freeing of the self, a delight in being unbounded, that comes with the recounting of the "I" experience in words carefully chosen and curated in a narrative of self.

As scholars of humanity, of society, of relations, we know that narrative is fundamental to the social self; "we are *homo fabulans* because we interpret and tell stories about who we are or want to be, and what we believe."[23] We might stretch to accept that narrative, perhaps including autoethnography, is fundamental to knowing about the social world. But I feel that the connection between my professional self and my social world is still tenuous. We swallow down so much of our selves to perform professionalism, and we do not yet admit how so many of our professional practices—the crafting of a journal article, the drafting of a funding bid, or promotion application—are practices of narration. We

---

[21] Morgan Brigg and Roland Bleiker, "Autoethnographic International Relations: Exploring the Self as a Source of Knowledge," *Review of International Studies*, 2010, 36(3): 779–798, p.789.

[22] Brigg and Roland Bleiker, "Autoethnographic International Relations," p.796.

[23] Annick Wibben, *Feminist Security Studies: A Narrative Approach* (London and New York, NY: Routledge) 2011, p.43.

are required, frequently and forcefully, to give accounts of our selves, but not accounts that admit the tensions and compromises that I have documented here; these tensions and compromises are remembered, rather than written, and are thus constituted as private, to be silenced.[24] In the accounts that are validated, the selves that are constituted are stable, whole, and coherent entities that perform and are performed by an illusion of certainty. "In our sanitised, self-evacuated, academic landscape, we become the 'hideous beings swallowed up by our scholarly clothes, the dancing fools under the fluorescent lights of our paradigms and theories that voraciously consume our thoughts, hammer the soul from our words, and drain our voices of any traces of humanity'."[25] There is no such illusion here.

I suspect that the political purchase of elaborating on research as a gendered intervention is to show that illusion of the chimera that it is. Such an act of resistance is in service of the transformation of the academy into a space of humility, uncertainty, and hope in spite of these things. There is little hope to be found when all questions have been answered and all possibilities exhausted. Identifying the performative practices through which I am constituted and exploring these practices as a narrative account of my self contributes to a vision of the social world that is not fixed and closed, but in the process of becoming, where possibility is very much alive.

The second dimension of political transformation stays with Elizabeth Dauphinee's question of ethical scholarship and extends the imbrication of the self in research to a consideration of context: what is the nature of the social world that we produce through our research encounters, our professional encounters more broadly? I face, am constrained by, and am constituted through, myriad technologies of power in my immediate institutional context: the way I must account for myself in a grant application, or conduct myself in a senior management meeting, or submit my syllabus for review and inspection. Each of these configures my academic world as a collection of successful and productive individuals, for this is how I am disciplined in the academy to think of my self. We compete (for funding), we evaluate each other (often harshly), we protect and hold close our academic judgments (in

[24] Elizabeth Dauphinee, "The Ethics of Autoethnography," *Review of International Studies*, 2010, 36(3): 799–818, p.805.
[25] Roxanne Lynn Doty quoted in Dauphinee, "The Ethics of Autoethnography," p.808.

both teaching and research), and we hide our failures from our selves and each other. The university in late modernity delights in the fiction of academic staff as functionally equivalent units, and fosters the growing sense of individualization, neglect, and loneliness that results in the growing numbers of people leaving the academy, or staying within and being broken by a system that insists it is a meritocracy, and therefore if there is a shortcoming or flaw it resides within the individual. This is a lie. And it is a lie not because we, as individuals, are not flawed, but because we, as individuals, must relinquish our social bonds, our affective relationships with each other and our many others—those with whom we interact in research, in parks, in pubs, and in lecture theaters—in service of the flexibilization of labor and commodification of knowledge in the neoliberal academy.

The neoliberal academy cannot quantify the bonds that support and sustain us as scholars. It cannot comprehend the connective tissue that binds us as a community, even as we bicker and quibble and are generally disagreeable with each other. It cannot recognize or value the collaborative, social, and the relational dimensions of our worlds. So this is the second point of political purchase: I tell this story to draw attention to how I am saved as a scholar, as an "I"-being, by acknowledging those bonds, and protecting—in word and deed—that connective tissue. I need to narrate my self in relation to my multiple others, in relation to our encounters, in order to understand the quality and texture of those connections, and to understand how they will continue to nourish me. This is a transformation of community: to ask that we as a community nurture and nourish each other not only in an abstract sense, by practicing hope and kindness, but in the very concrete sense of recounting—or accounting for—our selves as we are constituted in our encounters and how, as such, we are—I am—never individual, never alone.

Chapter 4

Engagement

I have spent all day here, in this slightly grubby room in a flat-roofed building on the outskirts of Brighton, having my first adventures in microfiche.[1] *The light is poor, and there is a knot between my shoulders. It is August 2002. Outside it is hot and bright, and I want to go and sit on the sun-warmed stones of the beach and drink vodka, lime, and soda, and stare endlessly at the sea. Instead, I scroll through the plasticky film searching for news articles about the Mothers of the Plaza de Mayo in Argentina, a process I will eventually learn to call "data collection." I want to understand more about how the Mothers of the Plaza de Mayo and the Greenham Common Women's Peace Camp deploy discourses of motherhood in their self-representation. I identify these women as activists, and their organization as a social movement. I am determined to understand them within the framework of IR, this strange discipline that I have begun to call home, but I perceive such a separation between their world and mine—not just a temporal divide but a gap of substance, where theirs is a praxis, a politics of the real, and my amateurish analytical writing is ephemera. They are not me. I am not them. I am not even close to that world. This shames me for reasons I don't quite understand.*

---

[1] This is a lightly edited version of an essay previously published as: Laura J. Shepherd, "Activism In/And the Academy: Reflections on 'Social Engagement'," *Journal of Narrative Politics*, 2018, 5(1).

And then, I am six or seven years old. Mum parks our 2CV on the slop-
ing tarmac of Sainsbury's car park, and I slide out of the back. It is cold;
I breathe into the scarf that mum has lent me, and it releases the ghosts of
her perfume, a scent memory the echoes of which to this day comfort me.
We walk past women shaking yellow plastic buckets, raising money to
support the miners in the north of England who were striking in protest
against mine closures. I knew only a little of this and had only a tenuous
grasp on what was at stake in the strike, but I knew that Thatcher was
bad, and unions were good, and solidarity was a virtue, so I asked mum
for some coins to put in the bucket on the way out. The metal warmed in
my hand as we approached, releasing that ferrous smell peculiar to hot
coins. I dropped the coins in the bucket, and they gave me a badge—red,
with white writing, I think—and I was pleased with myself for this per-
formance of politics. The strike ended in 1985, the Conservative govern-
ment proceeded with its program of economic liberalization, thousands
of jobs were lost and whole communities were impoverished as a result
of pit closures. I didn't often think about the miners' strike again.

And then, I am walking down the middle of a country lane near Laken-
heath, in the east of England. The lane is in shadow, almost fully, from the
tree branches that meet overhead. The air smells green. It is 1986, and
my dad and my stepmother have brought me on this march, a demonstra-
tion against the US bombing of Libya ordered by President Reagan on
the basis of Libyan involvement in several terrorist attacks on Americans.
There is a US airbase at Lakenheath. It is surrounded by a chain-link
fence; on our side of the fence, there is a gentle hill. I and a few other kids
spend the day rolling down the hill and crashing gently into the metal.
We sing "Don't bomb . . . bomb Libya" to the tune of the Frog Chorus,
and I have only the vaguest notion of where Libya was and no clue at all
about why it might be bombed. I am pleased because my best friend Joe
is there. Later we go back to his house, and his mum makes chapattis, and
we play in his garden, among the veggie patches and the apple trees, and
I mostly forget about Lakenheath, and Libya, and little kids playing at a
political protest in the shadow of the so-called Cold War.

And then, it is 2017. I got an email from a colleague in London,
with whom I'd planned to meet at the International Studies Association
annual convention in Baltimore, asking: Are you still going? Are you
boycotting? Which side are you on? I was the program chair for the

Feminist Theory and Gender Studies section, and it hadn't occurred to me that a boycott was possible. Other women, colleagues of a different kind, were simultaneously trying to work out how to support the women who would be traveling to New York for the Commission on the Status of Women in March, because the Women's International League for Peace and Freedom traditionally sponsors a delegation of women peace activists from the Arab world who wouldn't have been allowed into the country had the travel ban introduced by the Trump administration stood. But I hadn't connected the ISA convention to CSW. I don't boycott, in the end, but I do participate in the protest against the ban—against Trump's presidency, if we're being honest—standing outside the convention hotel, holding a sign and taking up space. It probably achieves nothing, but I feel almost part of something, a corporeal and substantial politics. It feels real, though I still feel like an imposter.

These stories give an account of politics as the occupation of public space: the picket line, the protest march, and the gathering of like-minded people to express dissatisfaction and dissent. This was the concept of activism I held when I entered the academy: "activism" as demand on one's time and one's body, an embodied performance of politics requiring sustained commitment, and organization, and coherence. This is the vision of activism in which I still struggle to see myself. This is the background against which I offer some thoughts about activism, and the academy, and the process of "social engagement."

A series of connections has informed my thinking about these concepts, the first of which is a relationship between activism on the one hand and scientism on the other. In this chapter, I explore the constitution of activism in the contemporary academy, examining its relationship to science—the work of even the *social* scientist—and the web of connections that link activism, scientism, authority, knowledge, and expertise. All of these are imbricated in contemporary discourse about social engagement, and I conclude with a discussion about the shift I believe we are witnessing in the constitution of academic subjectivity in the neoliberal academy. The subject now emerging from discourses about performance, relevance, and impact is an activist-scientist subject, and more besides. She is an expert, authority, and knowledge, yet the conditions of her possibility are restlessness, inadequacy, loneliness, and fear.

These two concepts, activism and scientism, exist in uneasy parallel, skittering in my mind like objects of opposite polarity: as a child,
I would play with small magnets, convinced that I could force the dull
dark gray rectangles to overcome the resistance that refused to allow
them to meet with a satisfying click. Scientism and activism in International Relations have similarly seemed mutually repellent at times,
getting close but never actually connecting.

This apparent inability of scientism and activism to merge in a
meaningful and productive way is, I think, grounded in the history of
the discipline of IR and its fetishization of (a particular configuration
of) science. As noted in the previous chapter, science is "a notion to
conjure with in the field of IR."[2] Scientism lauds such conjuring: ours
is conventionally a discipline of abstraction, hypothesis-testing, and
quantification of the social world, in the name of "rigor" and "objectivity." It is particularly this claim to objectivity that sticks with me as I
attempt to think through and around the scientism/activism relationship.
To be objective is to be scientific: to be scientific is to be objective. But
stowing away inside objectivity is a whole nested arrangement of values
and judgments that affect—and effect—how science is evaluated and
scientists (re)produced, primarily among which are notions of authority
and expertise.

Both authority and expertise are, of course, gendered. Gendered
ideas and ideals, assumptions that we hold about bodies and behavior,
inform (and are in turn informed by) dominant conceptualizations of
both expertise and authority. These concepts are tricky and unstable
things. Both expertise and authority are constituted through race, class,
coloniality, gender, sexuality, age, and multiple other identity markers,
and this has implications for how expertise and authority are embodied,
how experts and authorities *live* in the world, and how their expertise
and authority are received. We are conditioned to view dominant social
groups as experts, because those are the people to whom media outlets
turn when seeking an opinion on this event or that tragedy: their view is
privileged, and their subjectivity erased as they, through their positioning, speak for *all* people, not just particular (white, male) people.

With expertise, therefore, come the authority and the ability to speak
objectively, rather than subjectively, on a given topic. To provide

---

[2] Patrick T. Jackson, *The Conduct of Inquiry in International Relations: Philosophy of Science and Its Implications for the Study of World Politics* (London: Routledge) 2010, p.9.

an objective evaluation of a given situation—to perform *expert* and *authority*, in line with expectations—is to produce a distance between the speaker and the subject, such that the subject of exposition is not infected with the speaker's ideas, ideals, and values. "In standard practice," as John Law comments, objectivity "is usually detachment. Disentanglement from location."[3] Feminist critiques of objectivity in research are particularly relevant here, because part of feminist research practice relies precisely on attachment, entanglement, and the imbrication of the self in the research encounter. Feminist engagements with research values, and the values of positivist social science more broadly, question its fundaments in piercing and productive ways.[4]

These values, and the value ascribed to these practices, cohere in positivist IR research which insists on a sharp distinction between facts and values. Science, which produces facts, is value-free, or at least value-neutral, which is why IR as a knowledge domain for many years eschewed the idea of normative theory.[5] Learning about the philosophy of science in my PhD program, I struggled endlessly to make sense of the claim that theory could be value-free, "non-normative": how could one possibly sustain the idea that any account of the world could some-how be viewed solely in terms of what *is* and not recognized as a claim regarding what *should be*?

I never found peace with this struggle. As I began to form my own self-image as a researcher, I carved out a research space from which to disavow the scientistic dislocation demanded of me and espoused instead a research ethic that not only accepted my lack of objectivity but did not, in the first instance, perceive it *as* a lack. Instead, a feminist

---

[3] John Law, *After Method: Mess in Social Sciences Research* (London: Routledge) 2004, p.68.
[4] Joan Acker, Kate Barry, and Joke Esseveld, "Objectivity and Truth: Problems in Doing Feminist Research," *Women's Studies International Forum*, 1983, 6(4): 423–435; Kim V. L. England, "Getting Personal: Reflexivity, Positionality, and Feminist Research," *The Professional Geographer*, 1994, 46(1): 80–89; Sharlene, Hesse-Biber, "Feminist Research: Exploring, Interrogating, and Transforming the Interconnections of Epistemology, Methodology, and Method," 2–26 in Sharlene Nagy Hesse-Biber, ed., *Handbook of Feminist Research: Theory and Praxis* (London: SAGE) 2012.
[5] Mervyn Frost, *Towards a Normative Theory of International Relations* (Cambridge: Cambridge University Press) 1986; Chris Brown, *International Relations Theory: New Normative Approaches* (New York, NY: Columbia University Press) 1992; Mervyn Frost, "The Role of Normative Theory in IR," *Millennium: Journal of International Studies*, 23(1): 109–118.

research ethic is open about the situatedness of knowledge[6] and conscious of the ethical implications of such situatedness. Situated ethics are subjective by definition, and can be "characterized by the agent paying explicit attention to the particular situation and to the consequences for the relations between those involved, and by an absence of interest in making universal claims."[7] As per Law's comments quoted above, this willful entanglement of my self with my research put me at odds with the distance desired by the standards of my discipline, at odds with scientism writ large. As a scientist, I fail.

Thankfully, in this, at least, I have failed in good company. I completed my PhD research at an institution home to many academics who performed both scientism and activism, refusing the false dichotomy imposed by slavish devotion to the myth of objectivity, even seeking to "remake the mainstream . . . so that activist IR scholarship is the norm rather than the exception."[8] This was the culture within which I was formed as a junior researcher, an environment known for its critical mass of critical scholars and their shared commitment to decrying the nakedness of the emperor of science. Politics, which is what we studied when we studied together, was a politics of flux, of questioning the taken-for-granted and challenging the status quo. A politics of action, a politics of change.

Activism *requires* entanglement, ideals, total imbrication in a given social context, and the avowed situatedness of the self within a broader project of political change. This sense of politics-as-attachment permeated my developing academic consciousness, which was in turn already shaped by the exposure to political action I'd had as a child: mine was a childhood of Thatcher's dissolution of the Greater London Council, the *Socialist Worker*, "Free Mandela" T-shirts, and no South African oranges. Mine was a political consciousness of action, of doing, not

---

[6] Donna Haraway, "Situated Knowledges: The Science Question in Feminism and the Privilege of Partial Perspective," *Feminist Studies*, 1988, 14(3): 575–599.

[7] Bella Vivat, "Situated Ethics and Feminist Ethnography in a West of Scotland Hospice," 236–252 in Liz Bondi, Hannah Avis, Ruth Bankey, Amanda Bingley, Joyce Davidson, Rosaleen Duffy, Victoria Ingrid Einagel, Anja-Maaike Green, Lynda Johnston, Susan Lilley, Carina Listerborn, Shonagh McEwan, Mona Marshy, Niamh O'Connoer, Gillian Rose, Bella Vivat and Nichola Wood, eds, *Subjectivities, Knowledges, and Feminist Geographies: The Subjects and Ethics of Social Research* (Lanham, MD: Rowman & Littlefield) 2002, p.240.

[8] Eric Herring, "Remaking the Mainstream: The Case for Activist IR Scholarship," *Millennium: Journal of International Studies*, 2006, 35(1): 105–119, p.119.

of thinking. The space in the Venn diagram between activism and the academy seemed hard to access for me.

The etymology of activism derives from "activist," one who is committed to direct action in order to effect change. "Act" is thus central to the process of making sense of activism; derived from the Latin *actus*, "a doing; a driving, impulse, a setting in motion," an act is "a thing done."[9] There is a do-er implied in this configuration, an agent to act, and the materiality, or at least substance, of the "thing done." The activist is a do-er of things, a setter in motion of change according to the imperatives of their ethical framework, their politics. "In common parlance, activists are rabble-rousers, those who are *actually out there in the world* seeking to agitate, educate and direct political change."[10] The *world out there* is, implicitly, a different world than the world *in here*, the locus of academic life and scholarly endeavor.

Just as scientism inspires images of associative chains attaching science to, *inter alia*, objectivity, expertise, and authority, therefore, so too activism does invoke a series of conceptual connections, though of a different order. This is a constellation rather than a chain, a universe of related considerations that exceed the possibility of containment. Revolving lazily alongside the scientist/activist dichotomy spin a number of other binaries: active/passive; theory/practice; word/deed. These are binaries with which I have struggled throughout my academic career, and it is in the shadow of activism—in the space of theory, word, and *passivity*—that I have felt (perhaps still feel) most at home.

As I was completing the manuscript that would become the book presenting my doctoral research to the work, I wrote, in a somewhat snooty footnote which hopefully no one but the book's editor has ever read, that I perceive the "rigid separation" of theory and practice as "problematic."[11] I insisted on running the two words together throughout the book: mine was an account of "theory/practice." My obsession with practice was evident even in the title I settled upon for the book,

9 Online Etymology Dictionary, "act (n)," online at https://www.etymonline.com/word/act (accessed 12 February 2018).
10 Karena Shaw and R. B. J. Walker, "Situating Academic Practice: Pedagogy, Critique and Responsibility," *Millennium: Journal of International Studies*, 2006, 35(1): 155–165, p.157, emphasis added.
11 Laura J. Shepherd, *Gender, Violence and Security: Discourse as Practice* (London: Zed) 2008, p.176, Note 9.

which identifies "discourse as practice." I was, no doubt, protesting too much.

This derives in part from the philosophical position I developed in the book itself and which to the present day guides my encounters with the world: since reading Stuart Hall as an undergraduate student I have been obsessed with the politics of representation.[12] We apprehend the world through representational practice; as I understand it, there is no unmediated or extra-discursive "reality" that we can access—our words are our worlds, but also images, sculptures, textiles, and architecture are implicated in meaning-making. The meanings we make, and those representational practices through which we communicate, are fundamentally political, in that they are inextricably interlinked with power. Every claim to know is a practice of power, and every practice of power carries with it a claim to know. Power/knowledge, as Foucault has it,[13] is manifest in representation, and representation—including theory—is practice. This neat philosophical two-step allows me to collapse the space between word and deed—in theory, at least. But the residual uncertainty about the validity of this intellectual maneuver, the strange guilt I feel about identifying as a thinker, not a doer of things, persists, and colors brighten the perception I have of activism from the vantage point of my own gray, wordy, existence.[14]

Moreover, within the concept of activism there stows away a new configuration of expertise, different from the expert/authority of science but nonetheless influential and important to consider when exploring the relationship between activism and the academy.

---

[12] Stuart Hall, "The West and the Rest: Discourse and Power," 275–332 in Stuart Hall and Bram Gieben, eds, *Formations of Modernity* (Buckingham: Open University Press) 1992; Stuart Hall, "The Work of Representation," 13–74 in Stuart Hall, ed., *Representation: Cultural Representations and Signifying Practices* (London: SAGE) 1997.

[13] Michael Foucault, *Discipline and Punish: The Birth of a Prison* (New York, NY: Random House) [1977] 1995, 2nd edn, trans. Alan Sheridan, pp.27–28; Michel Foucault, *The Will to Knowledge: The History of Sexuality Vol. 1* (London: Penguin) 1988, trans. Robert Hurley, pp.92–102.

[14] This is of course not unrelated to the relentless drive for productivity imposed upon the subject in late modern capitalism. The production imperative is organized by the same logics that value "doing" over "being," measuring work ethic by output. These logics shape work practices in particular ways, with "the conspicuous display of busyness" becoming visible as a way to signal both virtue and status; Silvia Bellezza, Neeru Paharia, and Anat Keinan, "Conspicuous Consumption of Time: When Busyness and Lack of Leisure Time Become a Status Symbol," *Journal of Consumer Research*, 2017, 44(1): 118–138, p.121 and *passim*. I am grateful to Elizabeth Dauphinee for prompting me to reflect further on this connection.

Activists can claim a kind of "experiential authority," derived not from book-learning but from years of involvement with political struggle. In some fields, such authority underpins the identity category of "expert by experience";[15] per its straightforward formulation, this identity describes someone whose authority and credibility vis-à-vis a given issue comes from their lived experience rather than their years "prostrate to the higher mind," as the Indigo Girls would have it. The ascription of "expert by experience" in the context of activism presumes something about the authenticity and generalizability of experience, however, which is complicated. "What counts as experience is neither self-evident nor straightforward; it is always contested, and always therefore political."[16]

I have suggested that activism and scientism are frequently juxtaposed, but there is the possibility here of a shared foundation, stemming from the concept of expertise and the identity—the embodied presentation—of the expert. These are pressing concerns not only in the abstract but in the immediate political environment; ours at present is a world in which experts, and the evidence on which these experts draw to make their knowledge claims, exist within a mediascape populated by people who have "had enough of experts," per then-UK justice minister Michael Gove.[17] The relationship between experts and evidence is important, as is the relationship between experts and truth. Both scientists and activists use evidence and make truth claims: the differences here are a matter of degree, of tone, and shade. Neither the scientist nor the activist tends to question the existence of truth or the concept of evidence.

---

[15] "The social worker working with the expert by experience is suggestive of a relationship of equals whereby one expert's expertise has been accrued through their training and practice and the other through their experience"; see Hugh McLaughlin, "What's in a Name: 'Client', 'Patient', 'Customer', 'Consumer', 'Expert by Experience', 'Service User'—What's Next?" *The British Journal of Social Work*, 2009, 39(6): 1101–1117, p.1111. See also Tehseen Noorani, "Service User Involvement, Authority and the 'Expert-by-Experience' in Mental Health," *Journal of Political Power*, 2013, 6(1): 49–68; Jijian Voronka, "The Politics of 'People with Lived Experience': Experiential Authority and the Risks of Strategic Essentialism," *Philosophy, Psychiatry, & Psychology*, 2016, 23(3/4): 189–201.

[16] Joan W. Scott, "The Evidence of Experience," *Critical Inquiry*, 1991, 17(4): 773–797, p.797.

[17] Quoted in Julia Shaw, "The Real Reason that We Don't Trust Experts Anymore," *The Independent*, Friday 8 July 2016. Online, at http://www.independent.co.uk/voices/the-real -reason-that-we-don-t-trust-experts-a7126536.html (accessed 13 February 2018).

I, however, question both. Such questions belong properly to the philosopher, to the thinker of thoughts and not the doer of deeds, and in particular to those who—like me—are, by training, concerned about the organization of knowledge into seemingly immutable structures of capital-T Truth. We philosophers and thinkers, held as the enemy of the doers of deeds by many in the current "Knowledge Wars," are painted as wanton nihilists, indefensible relativists, intent on the destruction of all that is held to be good (and *true*). I question the things of which evidence is deemed to be evidence, and I question the things that are taken-for-granted in interpreting political life—among which I include the value of science and the benefit of activism. In the academy, at least, and in popular discourse to a significant extent, science has been elevated as a system of belief to the point where scientific truths have the status of unquestionable Truth and *it is no longer visible as a system of belief.* The desire, therefore, to point to this assumed value, the attribution of such a status to one mode of inquiry (scientific reasoning) to the exclusion of all others (affective, embodied, fictive, etc.[18]), is not the same thing as saying that all truths produced within this mode of inquiry are false or themselves questionable, but instead to make the rather different point that science itself functions as a particular *regime of truth* and that the politics, partiality, and potential problems with this ought to be borne in mind when wholeheartedly endorsing its knowledge as truth.

This position is alert to the ways in which evidence is marshaled in service of particular sets of arguments and the way that "common sense" ideas are invoked in order to foster and perpetuate particular formations of knowledge such that they become regimes of truth. But this means that I would use evidence to determine the credibility of a series of knowledge claims just like everyone else, while maintaining fidelity to the assumption that the credibility is contingent and conditional on the particular historical, social, and political context, as is the meta-level idea that "evidence" is the determinant of credibility (i.e., proceeding with the belief that actually existing facts are conditioned and produced by the fact-as-idea proposition in contemporary politics).[19] So in the realm of truth, as in the realm of science, I fail.

---

[18] Law, *After Method*, pp.2–3.
[19] That is, this thing is true because of science.

Do I fail as an activist? I think so, and not just because of my ambivalent relationship with Truth and my inability to commit acts of Truth to shore up my sense of expertise. Activism, in addition to requiring *action*, always seemed to me to require a degree of certainty I was unable to muster. So here, perhaps, is where scientism and activism meet after all: in the overlap in which resides a purity, a certainty, a burning righteousness that casts kaleidoscopic color on those within the radius of its radiance. Not I. Once, as a graduate student, I felt utterly and wholly deficient when I learned of a peer who worked for a prominent NGO as well as completing a PhD full-time. I remember asking my advisor whether it was true that research that didn't inform direct political action wasn't valuable research at all. My advisor assured me that my work was "real" work, that it was no less valuable a contribution for its attempt to speak to an academic rather than activist community, for its focus on words rather than deeds, for its theoretical purity and its lack of practical application. I remained (I remain) somewhat unconvinced. There is a residual insecurity at work here also, a suspicion that my advisor—my brilliant, sensitive, generous advisor—was lying me an alibi when she reassured me that mine was "proper" research.

"Imposter syndrome" is the condition that makes people doubt their expertise, despite their credentials; it makes people sit and second-guess themselves while others, though slower to reach the solution or find a contribution, put their hand up first. And while it affects everyone, it does not affect everyone equally: race, socio-economic background, and gender are significant. Women, for example, are far more likely to experience "imposter syndrome" than men; similarly, racialized scholars are also more likely to feel like imposters than their white peers in majority-white environments.[20] Both activism and scientism arouse the imposter in me. In neither domain do I feel "expert"; I would not claim either identity, and yet in the contemporary academy

[20] Julie King and Eileen L. Cooley, "Achievement Orientation and the Impostor Phenomenon among College Students," *Contemporary Educational Psychology*, 1995, 20(3): 304–312; Shannon McClain, Samuel T. Beasley, Bianca Jones, Olufunke Awosogba, Stacey Jackson, and Kevin Cokley, "An Examination of the Impact of Racial and Ethnic Identity, Impostor Feelings, and Minority Status Stress on the Mental Health of Black College Students," *Journal of Multicultural Counselling and Development*, 2016, 44(2): 101–117; Anna Parkman, "The Imposter Phenomenon in Higher Education: Incidence and Impact," *Journal of Higher Education Theory and Practice*, 2016, 16(1): 51–60.

the pressures brought to bear on academics to simultaneously perform both are significant.

When I had the conversation with my advisor, recounted above, I had no comprehension of "engagement," or "impact," or "knowledge transfer"; now these are ideas that have become commonplace in the neoliberal academy. I saw "activism" as one more pressure, one more underdeveloped dimension of my professional self, one more way to fail to meet the expectations others held. (I feel this no less keenly now, if I'm honest, but I perhaps have better defenses against that relentless, creeping feeling of inadequacy that seems to inhere in the academy.) A significant difference, however, between the academy as it was when I was but a neophyte and the academy as it is now, at least in the contexts with which I am familiar, is the expectation that activism—or at the very least "social engagement"—will be integrated into our work product, as part of our quotidian "responsibilities."

I consider my context to be both UK and Australian higher education. I am of, and embedded in, both of these cultures, which are divergent in so many ways; this causes some dissonance at times. But in the matter of "engagement," "impact," and "knowledge transfer," the logics are (perhaps unsurprisingly) similar. Far from the academy in the early 2000s, in which brilliant scholars had to fight to get their activism recognized as work, it is now the case—and again, this may be peculiar to the UK and Australia—that scholars who *don't* practice their politics have, in some sense, to account for themselves.

In the UK, research performance is measured every five years or so using the Research Evaluation Framework (REF; formerly the Research Assessment Exercise, or RAE). In 2014, the REF introduced research impact as a criterion of assessment, defining it as "an effect on, change or benefit to the economy, society, culture, public policy or services, health, the environment or quality of life, beyond academia."[21] This was the first time in the UK's highly bureaucratized and systematized research surveillance system that the "end-users" of research beyond the academy had been taken into account when determining the research performance of a given higher education institution.

Unsurprisingly, when the assessment criterion of "research impact" was made public, research administrators within universities across the

---

[21] Higher Education Funding Council for England, "REF Impact," no date. Online, at http://www.hefce.ac.uk/rsrch/REFimpact/ (accessed 14 February 2018).

UK began frantically to interrogate researchers about the "end-users" of, and "stakeholders" in, their research. Just as Alice passed through the looking glass into a world freed from conventional logics and behavior, so too did UK higher education transforms into a wonderland environment in which activism was not dismissed but instead valorized, even lauded. Written up into "impact case studies," the work that committed scholar-activists had been doing for years was suddenly of value to the academy and could be recognized *as* work, instead of fitted in to "personal" time.

This fundamentally changed the landscape of higher education in the UK. In Australia, where an impact assessment had been trialed two years earlier, the same dynamics are evident. To the scholarly workload of teaching and publishing was added a new category: engagement. Engagement is, apparently, the process through which research has an impact. Engagement is, in part at least, activism re-thought, activism in the garb and trappings of the neoliberal university. The process through which activism is commodified within the neoliberal university, though which value is ascribed to the political and politicized activity that previously would have been anathema to the value-neutral scientists of the ivory tower, transfers knowledge, through engagement, from the academy to society, such that research findings might have an impact on "the economy, society, culture, public policy or services, health, the environment or quality of life."

"Social engagement," as one Australian university strategy has it, "improves lives through advancing knowledge and understanding and with them, equality, diversity, open debate and economic progress."[22] This aligns with my own vision of the university as a public good. I am not drawing attention to this statement in order to criticize it, nor to suggest that it represents a flawed or otherwise lacking appreciation of how the university and its staff should interact with the society it serves. When preparing for my last promotion, in fact, I addressed the practice of social engagement directly; I discussed working with community organizations as partners in building knowledge networks, translating knowledge effectively for use by academic and non-academic stake-holders, and producing research that makes a difference in the world. I

---

[22] UNSW (the University of New South Wales), *UNSW 2025 Strategy: Our Strategic Priorities and Themes*, 2015. Online, at https://www.2025.unsw.edu.au/sites/default/files/uploads/unsw_2025strategy_201015.pdf (accessed 14 February 2018).

espoused a personal and professional commitment to ensuring that my research and teaching practice is informed by and in turn supports these values.

During the interview, I took a shallow breath and gave the example of my work in advocacy around Women, Peace and Security in Australia. I reported that I was a founding member of the Australian Civil Society Coalition on WPS and was, at the time, a member of the Coalition's Steering Group. I informed the committee that the Coalition was formed with the aim of keeping the government accountable and tracking progress on the implementation of the National Action Plan on Women, Peace and Security that we had developed from a very loosely defined group of interested people into a structured Coalition meeting regularly with the government. I said proudly that the engagement between the Australian government and the Coalition was held up as best practice in UN Women's 2015 Global Study on the Implementation of UNSCR 1325. I bit my tongue and commented that my work with the Coalition was representative of my enduring commitment to translating academic research for non-academic stakeholders and that I was proud to be supporting ongoing efforts to ensure that women across Australia have a voice in peace and security governance. I wore the costume of activism that day, activism derived from and mutually reinforcing the expertise I claimed as a scientist, a "leading" researcher in this field, and it served me well.

I explored in the previous chapter the seductive interpellative power of the subject of "expert" and the insecurities inherent in occupying that position, attempting to make sense for myself of the tension I feel in my role in the academy, which demands a performance of expertise from me even as I feel entirely unsuited to that subject-position. The root of my ambivalence toward the concepts of scientism and activism, as I have discussed, resides in an uneasy relationship with expertise. Discourses of expertise, engagement, and impact create subject-positions that are afforded value within the contemporary academy and they are subject-positions that feel ill-fitting to me.

I reflect on the fact that the research area where I focus most of my endeavors lends itself so well to the performances of expertise validated and rewarded by the university now; a knowledge economy of expertise has flourished in the field of Women, Peace and Security research, and there are so many consultancies, contracts, and opportunities for "engagement," for the work that we do to have "impact," it seems unbearable, like an admission of failure or defeat, to shy away from claiming that coveted position of "expert." We are an enterprise. I wonder wryly whether this is the approved collective noun for "experts" and whether I can bear to count myself among the number within the collective. I know that it would sting were I not to be counted by others as part of that community. I seem to occupy a liminal space, a space between those who are able to confidently claim recognition as experts and those who have no knowledge to transfer, no society to engage.

What might this say about the demands we place upon ourselves, the demands placed upon us as academics, within the academy today? I suggested that the pressure to "be active" was a pressure I felt keenly as I completed my doctoral research. The pressure I feel to "be scientific" in my inquiries is a pressure I feel confident and able to resist, but the pressure I feel to "be expert" is no less a weight upon me now, as I continue to conduct research that lends itself to "translation" for policymakers, bureaucrats, advocates, and (actual) activists in the sphere of Women, Peace and Security practice. I think this is the reason for my coming at the questions around activism and social engagement somewhat widdershins: in my current academic environment, the Australian/ UK higher education context I consider to be my academic home, the pressure comes from within and not without.

It is not society demanding engagement, it is the academy. It is not society demanding that we account for ourselves, share our expertise, perform relevance, *be active*, it is the academy. It is not solely our concern for international affairs that require we produce hot takes and op-eds and "conversation pieces" relevant to the contemporary political environment. Social engagement has been added, through measurement and reward and other forms of governmentality, to the plates we are required to keep spinning, the balls we are required to juggle. It is not enough to be an expert, however discomfiting "expert" might feel; we must be *relevant*.

I am reminded of Hans Christian Andersen's tale of the red shoes, some versions of which see the vain young protagonist dance herself to death in enchanted scarlet slippers. For the red shoes of relevance, we trade further, higher, expectations, alongside a diminished selection of acceptable objects of study. Just as a measurement of research performance that uses grant income as a proxy for quality quickly creates a massive influx of funding applications for any given scheme, and leads to a concomitant plummeting of success rates for that scheme, if the higher education sector and its research evaluation techniques are measuring research performance through social engagement and impact then researchers will self-select into areas that can most easily be fed into the engagement-impact Ouroboros.

I have a half-memory of being told by a Wiradjuri woman that in her language there is no word for "expert," because everybody is a custodian of some knowledge or another, and the idea that one quantum of knowledge would be valued over another, the idea that knowledge should be arranged in a fixed and immutable hierarchy, is faintly ridiculous. I try the thought of an academy without hierarchies and am returned to the start of this chapter, where I consider the relationship of science—surely the unifying logic of the academy if one is to be found—to expertise. How will we know if we are worth anything at all, if we cannot shield ourselves from the charge of irrelevance with our qualifications and our experience and our expert opinions?

I find it a perennial struggle, to express my occupation in a way that is descriptive but also that feels authentic. "I'm an academic"? Yes, that works, but a lot of people don't actually know what that means. "I'm a researcher"? True, for now, but too vague. "I'm a professor"? I can say that now, and I feel a certain thrill at claiming that promotion, but also too vague. "I work at the university" is vaguer still, and I am (for shame) disinclined to give up the prestige of my doctorate. "I study politics." This is closer. I try it on for size: "Mostly UN stuff, about gender and violence in conflict and post-conflict settings." That's ok. It works. It's not really what I do most of the time, but it sounds good. It sounds *relevant*. It sounds like a subject-position I can occupy without it slipping and chafing like ill-fitting (red) shoes.

This might not be enough, however, given the demand across the sector that academics claim expertise and pursue engagement. I do not like the effect that the uncritical celebration of expertise, engagement, and impact has on my community. In tandem with the hyper-individualization that the cult of expertise produces, demands for engagement contribute to the normalization of hyper-employment, especially for academics without job security. Those paid for teaching by the hour or by the course and those most precarious of colleagues whose routine exploitation is the oil that makes the motor of the academy run "engage" and perform their expertise for free, research in their own time, and receive no remuneration for their devotion to furthering knowledge, transferring knowledge from the academy to society; the assumption is that such devotion is its own reward or that it will ultimately reward the devotee with a permanent, continuing, position within the same academy that has been actively complicit in their exploitation for a year, or two, or ten.

The fact that academia is eating its young grieves me. I came through the job market in a different era but that was a case of luck, not judgment, so mine is a different story. But the grinding of brilliance to so much dust, the transfiguration of creativity and spark and wonder into performance metrics organized alphabetically in an Excel spreadsheet is the story of my community, and it is a tragedy. When reflecting on activism, engagement, and impact, I feel ill-prepared and inadequate, not expert enough to answer these questions; I also feel like these are not the right questions—the most relevant questions—to be asking at all. When I presented a version of this chapter at a conference, the discussant commented that I seem to be writing against my own sense of worthlessness, that this is an essay—owing much to the French etymology of the word here—against ephemerality. Negation is indeed a recurrent motif, a patterning, or a logic that gives shape to these paragraphs; I am not sure what it is that I am trying to erase other than my own doubts, fears, and wild imaginings.[23]

Perhaps there could be a more substantial foundation from which to reach for the constellations of recognition as "expert" than this iterative negation. Perhaps "engagement" can be differently configured/perhaps the fetishization of Science and Truth can be unbound, perhaps the pressures and tensions experienced by those subjected to the demands of the new academy can abate or at least be borne collectively, in a way that nurtures and values each of us but especially our most precarious, our most vulnerable. But in the face of that, which I obviously cannot know, all I have by way of defense against the abiding, grating anxiousness that grows from that space between activism and the academy is my narration, whatever meager words I can conjure in my effort to elaborate—to engage.

---

[23] I am so grateful to Naeem Inayatullah for his valuable and encouraging insights, both on this chapter specifically, and in general.

Chapter 5

Experience

Even as I'm walking, I'm writing; I'm working with words as the tides wash and whisper around me and I'm caught in wondering why the waves pull at my heart, deeply and directly. All my adult life I have wanted to live within walking distance of the ocean, to be able to wander down to the water's edge and soak in the sounds and the dampness of the briny air. This yearning is inexplicable to me, but the shoreline is my heart's home, and I know this as well as I know anything in the world. I didn't grow up by the sea. I was born in South London in 1977 and spent the first decade of my life there. I have memories of water, of holiday heat and beach tar and fresh peaches on the sand, of pebbles and softening ice-cream cones and the tightening of the skin on my nose as a gift from the surprisingly fierce British summer sun, but these are exceptional, not every-day, experiences and so I am at a loss to explain how and why I feel drawn to the cool salt endless ever-changing blue. I doubt who I am, often, doubt what I create and how I connect and whether I can truly know with certainty anything beyond this core truth of my world: I belong here. And every encounter that I have with the sea affirms this insight and every time I consider turning away, taking a different path, I am compelled to stay.

I don't know what else I might know with the same surety as this. My memories shift kaleidoscopically as I try to bring them into focus; I feel like I am over-writing, always, the space of recollection, reconstructing or constructing anew the ways I experienced this or that event or encounter. I am an unreliable witness in my own life. And I am

Broken Shell, Receding Tide. Photo by author.

ambivalent, in any case, about writing from experience as the foundation of truth, even as the erasure of experience inherent in the writing of that ambivalence sits leaden in my stomach and fills my throat. What violence do I do if I cannot permit within my architectures of knowledge claims to know from experience? I hang my head in shame.

But . . . but . . .

> *"I . . . don't know if I feel comfortable with you writing about trans lives."*
> *"Oh but we're not! We're writing about cis privilege. I mean . . . that's our positionality, right? We have to acknowledge it, open it up to critical scrutiny. Obviously, we can't assume anyone else's experience but we can explore our own experience, our own privilege. Maybe we even have a responsibility to explore that privilege."*
> *"I . . . guess? Sure."*

But . . . but . . .

This exchange never happened, or perhaps it did. I feel like perhaps I had a version of this conversation with a colleague, back in 2009 or 2010, when Laura Sjoberg and I were in the process of researching and writing our chapter on cis privilege in security politics, or maybe I have conjured it from the ghosts of my shame. The memory of its potential fills my mouth with the taste of old copper, even now, a decade later. This was—or was it?—my first collision with reflecting on *whether* I should write, a question apart from the more familiar questions of what, or how, or when I should write. I circled this question then and I find myself still wearing tracks around this question today. It brings to mind the worn dust paths around the edge of the fields where I used to ride horses at the weekends; the green is in between, and the path is bare of life. How do I deliberate the question of whether I should write? What does that question carry within it?

I never meant to hurt, or dismiss or trivialize the concerns of, my interlocutor, but that is not enough. Is it? Is it enough to side-step the concerns of those who live—who are positioned—at the fraying edges of safety, of comfort, of recognition, by saying glibly *But . . . but . . . These are my stories too.* How different is this claim from the sharp cry of an outraged toddler who wants the last biscuit or a different toy, specifically the toy in which another is delighting? *I want . . .* I want to be able to write and speak of matters of which I have no experience. That is the beginning and end of it. My academic career has been built on pontificating about matters of which I have no—or very little—experience. This book, in fact, is the first radical departure from that model, and after five chapters I remain unconvinced that it is going well. I have written always with the shiniest, clearest, most elevated of intentions, but that is not good enough. Or is it? *But . . . but . . .*

What would I have written about if I wrote only what I know, only that of which I have direct and personal experience? I would not have written about peacebuilding in Burundi, or Sierra Leone, nor about opportunities for women in "post-conflict" Afghanistan, nor about negotiating institutional change at the United Nations Headquarters in New York. I would not have trained in anthropology, nor international relations, nor political science. I would have, I suspect, followed my first instinct when I returned to the academy for graduate school and enrolled in a social work program. I watched my mother work her whole life to make the world better and safer and more accommodating for vulnerable children, and we too had moments of vulnerability, of unsafety; I lived, and so could presumably train in mitigating, the disruption, the air of violence, the curtailment of opportunity, and diminishment of agency that disproportionately affect women and their children when relationships break down. But I am not brave in the face of violence; even the mildest of conflict travels electric to my stomach and all of me wants to hide and all of me wants to smooth it over, to diffuse the situation, dissipate the crackling energy, to let it go to earth without exploding. And it would have destroyed my heart. I do not have the courage to show up for bruised and abused children day after day after endless horrifying days. I have been too much undone by the pain of others, unable to get out of bed for days, flattened by the awareness of so much suffering in the world. My boundaries are too porous to survive this work, even now.

I could write of being a woman. Women's and gender studies was another contender for graduate study when I was considering what program might suit me, before I landed on the Masters of Gender and International Relations at the University of Bristol, which was, at the time, the only program of its kind available in the UK; it was a fortunate find in so many ways but not least because (a) I could afford the fees and (b) I could afford the commute—both in terms of actual financial cost and in terms of disruption to my work schedule, necessary so I could manage the actual financial cost—to Bristol three days a week from the tiny Devon village where I was living at the time. I suspect I would have been happy enough reading feminist theory and intellectualizing women's oppression. That's not so different a life to the life I have now, some days. And I would have enjoyed teaching women's and gender studies, I think, learning with students how to identify and unthink and work against oppressive practices, connecting anti-sexist with anti-racist, anti-capitalist work, challenging bigotry and exclusions. Again, not so different a life from the life I have now. And I have learned so much from women's and gender studies that I feel compelled to pay my intellectual dues anyway, to continue to acknowledge how influential those scholars who opened up questions of identity for me as an undergraduate student have been on how I encounter the world now.

When I teach international relations, I teach gender studies anyway, and colonization, and community, and love. I teach as if it's unthinkable that we wouldn't center these things. I ask students to read bell hooks, and Lila Abu-Lughod, and Patricia Hill Collins, and I ask them to think with me about how power is distributed and how we can trace its effects. I ask them to read these works alongside their IR theory texts and to see how we can put these wildly different imaginings in conversation, to see what happens when we focus on relationality and the politics of representation in our explorations of sovereignty, for example. I encourage students to locate, and live, their experience in world politics, to connect and work with theory by understanding theory as a manifestation of experience—to make visible theorists as those whose thinking helps us make sense of and order the world. We read Marysia Zalewski together and together we sit with her idea that theory "is a way of life, a form of life, something we all do, every day, all the time."[1] In my teaching, I try to center experience; we read, and we talk, and I believe that we can build both community and understanding in our engagement with the world.

My own journey is one of trying resolutely to understand the position from which I speak, to fearlessly examine the relationship between identity and political consciousness in a way that feels authentic to the experiences I have had without being constrained by those experiences. I am reminded of one of many terrible poems I wrote as an undergraduate student, which began

I am a fragment
I am a woman
I am an absence of light

Much hinges on "I am"—personally, and politically. *I am* momentarily distracted by the presumed distinction between person and politics but perhaps it is not a distraction at all. I do not know how to conceive of my self if my self is not a political construct, put into discourse as a composite of all *I am* assumed to be, interpreted as, embodying. And what of my body? I am feeling my way to safety in my skin, but this is fragile and new to me, not to be trusted. Perhaps I have had few qualms moving away from materialist theory because I have lived so dis-integrated, so dis-connected from my own corporeality. Easier to occupy a "place that is unknown and risky . . . a place of discourse from which

---

[1] Marysia Zalewksi, "All These Theories Yet the Bodies Keep Piling Up: Theory, Theorists, Theorising," 340–353 in Steven Smith, Ken Booth, and Marysia Zalewski, eds, *International Relations Theory: Positivism and Beyond* (Cambridge: Cambridge University Press) 1996, p.346. See also: Brooke A. Ackerly, "Women's Human Rights Activists as Cross-Cultural Theorists," *International Feminist Journal of Politics*, 2001, 3(3): 311–46; Laura J. Shepherd, "Whose *International* is it Anyway? Women's Peace Activists as International Relations Theorists," *International Relations*, 2017, 31(1): 76–80.

speaking and thinking are at best tentative, uncertain, unguaranteed"[2] than to rehabilitate my relationship with my body in service of my feminist politics, I suspect. Easier to disavow the substance of my place in the world than to own the ways in which my whiteness, femininity, heterosexuality, middle-class British accent, and physical form structure my encounters and how I am in turn encountered.[3] Amid these markers of identity, where do I stand? How do I—can I—elaborate my stand/point?

I struggle with experience, and standpoint, as ways of knowing. A standpoint epistemology suggests that the standpoint of the "knower" is of primary importance to the construction of knowledge and "carries with it the contention that there are some perspectives on society from which, however well-intentioned one may be, the real relations of humans with each other and the natural world are not visible."[4] The lived experiences of an individual subject construct a certain way of accessing the world, of knowing, which then functions as a way of knowing in a system within which certain knowledges are privileged over others. Disadvantage, inequality, and harm produce insight into structures of oppression, exclusion, and discrimination.

But I turn over and over again the question of what stability is presumed when knowledge claims are articulated on this basis. Feminists have sought to articulate a feminist standpoint epistemology to "legitimate women as knowers,"[5] arguing that the standpoint of women, constructed as it is by the experiences of women as oppressed subjects in a patriarchal society, validates their knowledge over knowledge produced from alternative standpoints. The justifications for this epistemological claim are "based on the many differences between the situation, lives

---

[2] Teresa de Lauretis, "Eccentric Subjects: Feminist Theory and Historical Consciousness," *Feminist Theory*, 1990, 16(1): 115–150, p.138.

[3] Judith Butler suggests that "[t]he theories of feminist identity that elaborate predicates of color, sexuality, ethnicity, class and able-bodiedness invariably close with an embarrassed 'etc.' at the end of the list," a phrase which haunts me. Judith Butler, *Gender Trouble*, rev. edn. (London: Routledge) 1999, p.182.

[4] Nancy Hartsock, "The Feminist Standpoint: Developing the Ground for a Specifically Feminist Historical Materialism," 283–310 in Sandra Harding and Merrill B. Hintikka, eds, *Discovering Reality: Feminist Perspectives on Epistemology, Metaphysics, Methodology and Philosophy of Science* (Amsterdam: Kluwer) 2003, p.285.

[5] Sandra Harding, "Introduction: Is There a Feminist Method?," 1–14 in Sandra Harding, ed., *Feminism and Methodology: Social Science Issues* (Bloomington, IN: Indiana University Press) 1987, p.3.

and experiences of women and men,"[6] though these justifications are quiet on the matter of differences *among* women, which preoccupy me. The existence of a coherent and integrated knowing subject on whose behalf a political movement can claim rights is, so it is argued, logically a prerequisite of identity- or rights-based politics. Christine Di Stefano, for example, wrote in fierce defense of this position, arguing that "the post-modern prohibition against subject-centred enquiry and theory undermines the legitimacy of a broad-based organized movement dedicated to articulating and implementing the goals of such a constituency."[7] But I cannot wear comfortably the erasure of experience of difference, even as claiming authority from experience sits awkwardly on and in my body also.

I write this in troubled times for feminism (as if there was any other kind of times for a difficult, dissident, political project). Popular and public debates about feminist theory and gender politics are, while expressing concern for women's rights, making it clear that such rights cannot be claimed by *all* women; while paying lip service to the idea that plural feminisms can exist—articulating token validations of Black feminist thought, for example—attempting to delineate clear and unquestionable boundaries around *Real Feminism*™. *Real Feminism*™ includes emancipatory politics on behalf of women (but only *some* women, those determined as "born women" or "biological women") and excludes everything else. But this is not the feminism in my blood, of my body. My feminism, as Flavia Dzodan succinctly articulated, "will be intersectional or it will be bullshit."[8] Because *Real Feminism*™ and its subject of praxis has been contested from the start. Those theorists I read with my students, in our classes on world politics in which we imagine relations international-local-personal at the center of our thinking, write always and with all of their hearts against the notion that white feminism is *Real Feminism*™ despite its universalizing claims.

---

[6] Marysia Zalewski, *Feminism After Postmodernism: Theorising through Practice* (London: Routledge) 2000, p.51.

[7] Christine Di Stefano, "Dilemmas of Difference: Feminism, Modernity and Postmodernism," 63–82 in Linda Nicholson, ed., *Feminism/Postmodernism* (London: Routledge) 1990, p.76.

[8] Flavia Dzodan, "My Feminism Will Be Intersectional or It Will Be Bullshit," *Tiger Beatdown*, 10 October 2011. Online, at http://tigerbeatdown.com/2011/10/10/my-feminism-will-be-intersectional-or-it-will-be-bullshit/.

Real Feminism™ has never had a stable subject on whose behalf to claim rights. There have always been inclusions and exclusions. In Leslie Feinberg's novel *Stone Butch Blues*, which shattered my heart in so many ways, I was struck by the scene in which Theresa reports being excluded from a lesbian rights group on campus—despite being a lesbian—because she was in love with a butch:

> "They told me that butches were male chauvinist pigs!"
> I knew what male chauvinist meant, but I couldn't figure out what it had to do with us.
> "Don't they know we don't deal the shit, we get shit on?"[9]

And this is the point, for me. Some of us (many of us) are occasionally in a position to deal with the shit—sometimes, precariously—but we also get shit on. As a group, those assigned female at birth have historically and repeatedly been marginalized, excluded, violated, and harmed. As a group, people whose gender presentation doesn't conform to their sex assigned at birth have also historically and repeatedly been marginalized, excluded, violated, and harmed. There has to be room in my feminism to support both those groups of people, because rigid and regulatory societal gender norms are the problem here; my feminist politics has been a journey of learning how best to understand and mitigate the damage of those norms. Because enforcing those norms causes harm, I move like water toward instability, uncertainty, and partiality. Perhaps still after all these years, *I am a fragment*. Perhaps

> We can learn how to embrace the instability of the analytical categories; to find in the instability itself the desired theoretical reflection of certain aspects of the political reality in which we live and think; to use these instabilities as a resource for our thinking and practices.[10]

Standpoint theorising collapses for me at the point at which it insists upon a universal position from which to speak, a unification of diversity with homogenizing and often violent ends. But how do we learn, and know, if not from reflecting—raising consciousness—of our own

---

[9] Leslie Feinberg, *Stone Butch Blues* (Ithaca, NY: Firebrand Books) 1993, p.135.
[10] Sandra Harding, "The Instability of the Analytical Categories of Feminist Theory," *Signs: Journal of Women in Culture and Society*, 1986, 11(4): 645–664, 648.

experience? What evidence can we marshal and what is the basis of our claims, if not evidence of experience, a life or lives made meaningful, sensible, and charted? I am endlessly intrigued by the question of evidence, tied so closely to the disciplinary practices to which we are subjected if we journey through the academy.

I am interested in disciplines and fascinated by disciplinary transgression. I was trained in the disciplinary conventions of social anthropology at the undergraduate level. Anthropology as a discipline is highly reflexive, resistant to abstraction, and aware of the politics of representation and positionality. Back in the 1970s, anthropologist Annette B. Weiner was undertaking field research in the Kiriwina Islands of Papua New Guinea (then known as the Trobrian Islands), with a view to unsettling disciplinary notions of common sense regarding gender neutrality of ethnographers and challenging the disciplinary canon in profound and influential ways.[11] My postgraduate training in the discipline of international relations was, therefore, a curious through-the-looking-glass adventure in double-think. Having been disciplined into thinking interpersonally, specifically, and contextually, always accounting for my own subjectivity in my tentative conclusions, always alert to the operations of (gendered, racialized, and capitalist) power, the concepts and vocabulary of this strange discipline confounded me. The state, the balance of power, the security dilemma: I felt these were unwieldy thinking tools, impossible conjurings to work with, operating at a scale that was meaningless to me.

Even having received my disciplinary training and being settled in my new "home" discipline (so richly textured and evocative, the metaphor of "home" allows for all sorts of interesting variants such as Christine Sylvester's idea of camps[12] and homesteading[13]), I have historically not been terribly *well*-disciplined. As a feminist IR scholar,

---

[11] Annette B. Weiner, *The Trobrianders of Papua New Guinea* (New York, NY: Holt, Rinehart and Winston) 1988. This was the first academic book I ever read the whole of, and it largely motivated my decision to study anthropology as an undergraduate—which then affected which university I attended, which determined the people I met, and so on. This book, in the truest sense, changed my life.

[12] Christine Sylvester, "Whither the International at the End of IR," *Millennium: Journal of International Studies*, 2007, 35(3): 551–573.

[13] Christine Sylvester, *Feminist Theory and International Relations in a Postmodern Era* (Cambridge: Cambridge University Press) 1994.

the work I do was once pronounced marginal;[14] as my philosophical sympathies lie with poststructuralism, my work has been aligned with "prolix and self-indulgent discourse . . . divorced from the real world."[15] My encounters with my discipline have not been uncomplicated and it has provided me with plenty of material with which to think through the question of disciplinarity. I, along with many—if not most—other feminist IR scholars have experienced the assertion of disciplinary boundaries, and stood accused of disciplinary transgression: *It's very interesting . . . but is it IR?*

The idea of *a* discipline (noun), in the academic sense, clearly derives from the verb: both relate to establishing clear boundaries between what is right and good (behavior/research) and what is wrong and bad (behavior/research); both have ways to correct transgression when an uninitiated (or resistant) person strays. As academics, scholars, and educators, we are trained to recognize the boundaries of our discipline and to stay within them; historians don't usually apply for jobs as social workers just as creative writing majors don't generally win contracts for the redesign of shopping centers.

The problem is that the boundaries between "good" and "bad" behaviors are fiction. I do not mean that there are no boundaries, or that there shouldn't be any boundaries, but rather that we can always find the exception that confounds the rule. If I begin to worry at, to unpick or unravel, the tapestry of the rule, however, it becomes very difficult to defend or justify any point of principle at all, which generally makes people feel very uncomfortable. So when I say that the concept of discipline (in academia) is a fiction, I mean that it is *something held to be true because it is expedient to do so*. It *suits* us to believe in disciplinary boundaries, just as it suits us to believe that there are solid and

---

[14] I don't wish to belabor this point, as others more eloquent than I have already levelled convincing critique, but by way of context for the unfamiliar reader: in his 1996 article, which won the annual British International Studies Association award for best article published in the *Review of International Studies* that year, Adam Jones described the significance of feminist scholarship to the discipline of IR (and the issues, events, and phenomena with which feminist IR scholarship was concerned) as "marginal, if that word still retains its pejorative connotations." Adam Jones, "Does 'Gender' Make the World Go Round? Feminist Critiques of International Relations," *Review of International Studies*, 1996, 22(4): 405–429, p.417; see also Terrell Carver, Molly Cochran and Judith Squires, "Gendering Jones: Feminisms, IRs, Masculinities," *Review of International Studies*, 1998, 24(2): 283–297.

[15] Stephen Walt, "The Renaissance of Security Studies," *International Studies Quarterly*, 1991, 35(2): 211–239, p.223.

unbreakable rules about what is "good" and "bad" (which is why we have laws and so on).

These boundaries that we establish between little pockets of knowledge in the academy are a fiction. Being ill-disciplined, to my mind, is about challenging the fiction of disciplines, about recognizing that knowledge isn't something that can be carved up into neatly bounded parcels that we then work either *in* (to produce disciplinary knowledge); at the intersection *of* (to produce interdisciplinary knowledge); or *with* (to produce multi- or cross-disciplinary knowledge). Ill-disciplined work subverts the very foundations of the concept of "the discipline," resisting and transcending the always arbitrary and fictive boundaries between; borrowing from Foucault,[16] I suggest that talk of disciplines and disciplinary boundaries bring into being the categories themselves and such categories are always normative.

Michel Foucault's work on discipline specifically leads me further away from the idea that disciplines are neutral and administrative categories, implicating political economy in the concept of discipline: "Discipline increases the forces of the body (in economic terms of utility) and diminishes these same forces (in political terms of obedience)."[17] To be *useful* in contemporary society, one must be disciplined. Without discipline, we as subjects are of no use to the governing elite, to the institutions of governmentality with which he was also concerned.

Crucial to Foucault's analysis is the idea that, without disciplinary training, we do not learn to be functional (productive) members of society, and if we are not functional and productive members of society then we are a net cost. Put simply: the more obedient we are, the more useful we are. Our utility is directly proportionate to the extent to which we are disciplined. Foucault was, of course, writing about Anglophone Western society as a whole, not about academia specifically. It's clear to me, however, that the same disciplinary techniques are in place from primary school to the academy. Students are recruited and enrolled by the dozen into university programs, whereupon I collude with the managerial imperative to teach them what it means to "be" a scholar. Students stay with us for a year, or several, and during that time they have to submit hundreds of pieces of writing that must conform to

[16] Michel Foucault, *Discipline and Punish: The Birth of the Prison*, trans. Alan Sheridan (London: Penguin) [1975] 1977.
[17] Foucault, *Discipline and Punish*, p.138.

clearly delineated standards in order to pass. At the undergraduate level, even the taught postgraduate level, I offer in my course materials clear indications of the normalizing judgment employed in my teaching: "Upon successful completion of this course, you should be able to . . ." I choose textbooks carefully, mindful of the student's tendency to accept textbooks as the source of all truth, but cannot avoid communicating my version, my vision, of the basics of our discipline. I set exams and topics for research papers, I write learning outcomes, I teach students how to write evidence-based argument and to integrate theoretical discussion with empirical analysis. I offer up my students for evaluation by examination boards, which grant credit points to students that meet the stated requirements; students eventually accrue enough credit points to graduate and so they do.

Rarely, it seems, do many colleagues encourage students to question why they're doing what they're doing—and when such questioning is encouraged, when the conventional order of disciplinary training is challenged or subverted, it is seen as impertinent, troublesome, and *ill-disciplined*. When I put forward such questions, *I* am seen as impertinent, troublesome, and *ill-disciplined*.[18] Mostly, though, I perpetuate the narrative that they are at university to receive training in their discipline and that they will graduate as members of their discipline. Everything that I do as a scholar-educator eases this progression, even when I seek and craft spaces in which—from which—to trouble disciplinary structures of domination in my practice.

And at the heart of every discipline is its knowledge. Knowledge, so the adage goes, is power; at the heart of every discipline, then, is its politics of knowledge production. What counts as knowledge? How can we evaluate the credibility of a claim to know? In dance, a student can enact or perform technique for peers to judge. In mechanical engineering, a colleague might build a bridge from A to B and judge its structural integrity. In medicine, a disciplinary neophyte could diagnose a patient or carry out surgery and be judged on the accuracy of the diagnosis or the success of the surgical intervention. There are no such markers in the social sciences: we have only the strength of our arguments, and we measure that strength by its evidence base. There are fierce disagreements within our intellectual community over what counts as evidence

---

[18] Nevertheless, she persisted.

(does a presidential statement carry the same weight as an anonymous comment on a blog somewhere?); over whether claims to know are universal or particular; over whether knowledge is objective, subjective, or constituted as knowledge through the specific discursive conditions of its emergence. Further, whether our knowledge production is described as "hypothesis testing" or "storytelling," whether we offer our conclusions as one possible interpretation among many or as The Proven Truth—whatever our framing, what we are framing is evidence-based.

At the heart of the discipline of IR, there is a fetish for evidence, a fetishization of evidence-based argument. On this, implicitly or explicitly, IR scholars agree. I seek evidence in my own work—even this ill-disciplined series of reflections is littered with footnotes to scholarly texts, as I grasp at the wisdom of those who said what I said first and better—and I demand it from my students. "What is the basis of this claim?" I scribble in the margins. "You can't just assume that this is the case. What's your *evidence*?." "Disciplines" are constituted by their non-negotiables. They are fictive but given meaning through our continued invocation of them as meaningful categories. I have been taught how to behave in my intellectual pursuits and, while disciplines allow vigorous debate over ontological assumptions, epistemological positions and methodological choices, there are boundaries that cannot be transgressed without corrupting the notion of disciplinary belonging.

Roland Bleiker wrote a profound and brilliant paper years ago exhorting the discipline to "forget IR theory."[19] Perhaps the only way to deny the imperative of disciplinarity, to resist the straitening of horizons of possibility invested in disciplinary belonging, is to forget. In IR, I think that means problematizing the fetish for evidence and investigating how else I might construct a contribution to knowledge, if not a claim to know: autobiographic and autoethnographic accounts; art; fiction writing; poetry. This project, this writing here, today, feels like a project I have been circled toward elliptically over the past decades, writing my way closer to each more conventional essay written in a more conventional mode. I glance sideways at the evidence here, probing experience for a means of understanding, a means of connection—a way to lay bare the interwoven threads of my story with yours, theirs, ours. So perhaps I "forget IR theory," or write IR theory of a different order: theories of

---

[19] Roland Bleiker, "Forget IR Theory," *Alternatives: Global, Local, Political*, 1997, 22(1): 57–85.

the international, and of relations, and of theory, which tell different stories in different ways.

That said, I struggle with storytelling sometimes. Not (just) the practice, but the concept. It can feel ill-fitting, which is peculiar to me as I have written a lot about telling stories over the years. I think perhaps because I have re-engaged with the concept of storytelling not only in my teaching, learning from decolonial efforts to open up spaces of knowledge production, but also in my writing and in an attempt to bring that same sensibility, that same awareness to my writing I feel inevitable that I am failing, posturing, an imposter. I want to hold on to the concept of storytelling in my writing, to be guided by the theoretical assumption that "the form and content of the stories we tell are constituted by and constitutive of our world(s) and our place(s) within it,"[20] but I also want to acknowledge that leveraging storytelling as a concept can be a kind of appropriation, a violence in itself.

I was prompted to this thought by a brief introduction to a collection of essays on decolonization and Indigenous knowledge. I draw on this collection in my teaching, as I too seek "to disrupt Western imaginations of 'theory'" though only belatedly "through Indigenous knowledge production and storytelling," as the authors of the introductory essay lay out.[21] These authors, Aman Sium and Eric Ritskes, offer a meditation on storytelling that I invite my students to explore with me, beginning with the idea that the "word—'story'—is far too simple for the complex and rich understandings" that are manifest in the essays presented in the collection. They continue: "Stories in Indigenous epistemologies are disruptive, sustaining, knowledge producing, and theory-in-action. Stories are decolonization theory in its most natural form."[22] My mind catches, every time, on the binding function of epistemology here, drawing together experience and evidence in ways that diverge vertiginously from disciplinary expectations about knowledge production.

---

[20] Laura J. Shepherd, *Gender, Violence and Popular Culture: Telling Stories* (London: Routledge) 2013, p.11.

[21] Aman Sium and Eric Ritskes, "Speaking Truth to Power: Indigenous Storytelling as an Act of Living Resistance," *Decolonization: Indigeneity, Education & Society*, 2013, 2(1): i–x, p.ii.

[22] Sium and Ritskes, "Speaking Truth to Power."

The academy has often sanitized storytelling. I feel uncomfortably aware that I have been complicit in making storytelling palatable as a way of knowing by eradicating the traces of revolution it could have borne. Storytelling in the neoliberal academy is a cut flower in a pot of soil, wilting and malnourished. I am, of course, not the first to have taken up the question of how and why and with what effects we are working with—and diminishing—the concept of storytelling; my brilliant colleague Sujatha Fernandes has offered a political history of storytelling[23] that reveals the interpellation of the practice into rationalities of market and governance in ways that undercut the transformative potentiality signaled by Sium and Ritkes. Fernandes deftly demonstrates that the corporatization of storytelling—its incorporation into fundraising, advocacy campaigns, marketing, and all forms of politics—denudes stories of theory, of critique, of explanation: "the contemporary approach to storytelling by political strategists and consultants is one that privileges feeling and emotions, tying them to an amorphous notion of values that discounts a critique of macro structures and political analysis."[24]

Part of the politics at play here is the whitewashing of storytelling as an epistemology, as a way of taking experience as evidence and eviscerating those edifices of knowledge production that insist that it is invalid. While dominant scholarship might push aside methods such as autoethnography or traditional storytelling as not rigorous enough or as "identity politics," the experience of those who live out decolonization are integral to the integrity of the movement, grounding it to the material realities of the people whose lives bear the scars of colonialism and the long histories of resistance and triumph.[25]

The integrity of stories that matter, that *are* matter, is lost in the sea of vacuous expressions of self in story form; I am sometimes not convinced I am offering anything beyond that here, hence my repeated return to uncomfortable deliberation on this theme. The stories—and story *form*—that popularized storytelling, the academy and beyond, are too frequently "disembedded from their contexts and, as the relating of

---

[23] Sujatha Fernandes, *Curated Stories: The Uses and Misuses of Storytelling* (New York: Oxford University Press) 2017.
[24] Fernandes, *Curated Stories*, 33.
[25] Sium and Ritskes, "Speaking Truth to Power," iii.

isolated personal experiences, facilitate[] an individualizing of collective struggles."[26]

I am lost in, and without, and outside, storytelling. I am lost. But I have the privilege, the security, of being lost, and knowing I can fake it till I'm found. The experience I have accrued in the discipline affords me that much. I am positioned to tell my stories and have those stories heard. I am part of the problem here.

On the last day of the 56th Annual Convention of the International Studies Association, held in Baltimore, USA, in 2015, I tweeted: *So it's done. And that's something. #ISA2015 <mic drop>.* I was exhausted by that point, numbed and overwhelmed at the sheer volume of thoughts I had processed over the previous four days. I was ready to crawl into bed and sleep for a week, but I still had to get home, back to Sydney.

I stared unseeing out of the airplane window as we circled around Sydney, thinking about nothing much at all, noticing the Opera House

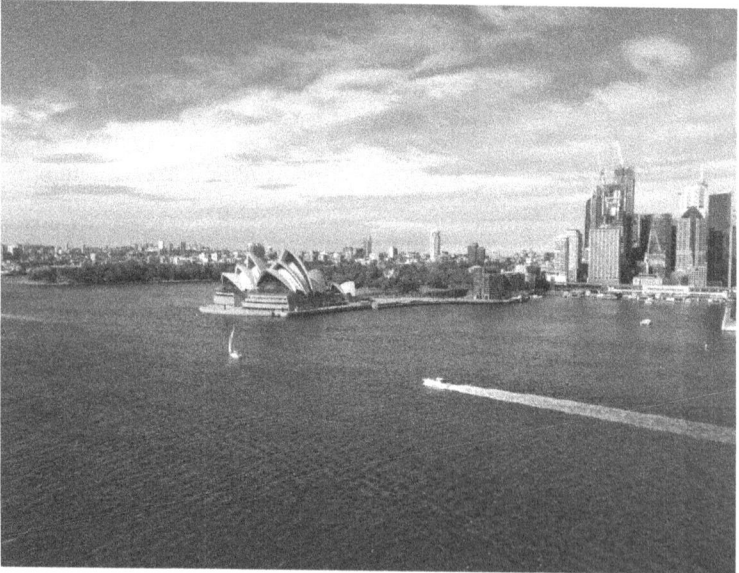

Sydney Opera House from Sydney Harbour Bridge. Photo by author.

---

[26] Fernandes, *Curated Stories*, 36.

and the Sydney Harbour Bridge and how tiny they looked, how much like models, how insignificant. In the taxi on the way home (and I am shamed by this extravagance), I asked the driver to please take the bridge, not the tunnel. There is something about the view from the Eastern Distributor, which brackets Circular Quay with the Harbour Bridge on one side and the Opera House on the other, that feels to me like coming home.

As we drove, and the iconic structures came into view, I thought, somewhat mindlessly, how much bigger they seemed close up. I was exhausted, not able to conjure much more than this rather banal observation. Objects in the rear-view mirror may be closer than they appear, but objects on the ground, when you're close up, feel much more significant.

It stuck with me, though, as I unpacked my suitcase and had coffee and hugged my husband and my child and had more coffee and began to work my way through the mountain of work that had accumulated in my absence. It stuck with me because it was kind of how I felt about the convention that year. It felt enormous, significant, like home, while I was right there, up close, breathing the same air; but from afar, it seemed tiny, and I was left wondering about the significance.

Before the convention, the association announced a series of four "featured" panels that they named the "Sapphire Series." Cynthia Weber wrote a brilliant critique of the series,[27] drawing attention to the dynamics of the performative perpetuation of white privilege, and a gathering of critical voices joined forces on social media to debate exactly how totally ignorant of racialized exclusion one would have to be to not notice that there wasn't a single person of color on any of the "featured" panels. There were discussions on blogs and on Facebook, and some rather wonderful tweets. The "featured" series went ahead as planned. I didn't go. It was a meaningless boycott, because I never intended to go. I went instead to the panels that nourish me, panels at which my smart feminist academic heroines present their smart feminist research. And I went to one Presidential Theme panel, "Feminist International Relations Today: Transformation in Action," in the "graveyard" slot (the final session of the final day of the convention).

This is the panel that links my musing about the relative size of the Sydney Opera House with my attendance at the ISA convention (and

---

[27] Cynthia Weber, "ISA's Sapphire Series—Is Blue the New White?," *Duck of Minerva*, 6 February 2015. Online, at https://www.duckofminerva.com/2015/02/isas-sapphire-series-is-blue-the-new-white.html.

thus my complicity in the performance of privilege that the convention constitutes). I'm not sure that I can yet, even years later, communicate the ways in which it was the most powerful, the most unsettling, the most difficult panel I have ever attended. Still now, many years later, I stretch my fingers over the keyboard of my laptop, drop my shoulders, and breathe deep into my belly, in an effort to disperse the discomfort I still feel in my body when I think about the event. Seated at the top table, which was draped as always in pristine white hotel linen, were four or five brilliant feminist colleagues, ready to speak—or so we thought—on "transformation in action." Instead, transformation was enacted. Riffing on the racialized exclusion of the Sapphire Series, the panelists performed their own exclusion, writing on the body of Swati Parashar—the only woman of color on the panel—the "difference" that the Sapphire panel organizers failed to see. Swati sat at the end of the table, positioned far from the white women passing the microphone among themselves; she was not introduced to the audience and was not invited to speak, while our colleagues deliberated on feminism, marginalization, and exclusion. Swati was ultimately so troubled by the feelings this treatment aroused in her that she departed the panel to stand at the back of the room, behind the audience, with her back to the wall. At this point, the performance broke down, unable to sustain the suspension of care (for individuals, for our community), the discomfort, and the shattering of expectations and beliefs.

Because of these acts—refusing to introduce Swati to the audience, the audience's refusal to countenance the continuation of debate without Swati's input, Swati's decision to take herself out of the privileged space allotted to the panel and to position herself physically on the margins of the debate—disrupted the space completely. It became clear that Swati's departure was not planned as part of the performance; it was a way of knowing/showing the politics of the encounter, a way of embodying knowledge of feminism, marginalization, exclusion. The audience could not cope. I could not cope. I hid behind my iPad, taking short clips of video and tweeting about the evident discomfort in the room.

When invited to speak, I spoke of shame. I was ashamed that the inadequacies of my professional association fostered an environment in which such a performance was necessary, to point out the lack of reflexive awareness of privilege and position. I was ashamed that I was not the first to move in solidarity with Swati when she opted out of her role on the panel. I was ashamed that I could not comfort the chair of the panel, who—despite having planned the performance in collaboration with the other panelists—was obviously deeply distressed by the events unfolding. I was ashamed that I named another scholar as an example of race-ignorance in the discipline. I still feel that I should not have done that. I was ashamed that all I could do was to stay in this space, participate in this discussion, admit to the feelings that participation aroused within me, and I was—I am—afraid that this was not enough.

And it is not enough. I am still ashamed. I feel I have done little more, or not enough, with this feeling. The performance of the panel, the discussion, the awakening of emotion and of our relationality with each other and with our discipline felt monumental—path-breaking, paradigm-shifting—close up. Now it feels tiny, and I feel tiny along with it. I still don't know what to do with these feelings. I don't know how to make these feelings stay monumental, how to ensure that they fill my intellectual space: my writing and my teaching, and my life. I should hold this shame in its enormity and let it color my engagement with my world. I do not know how to do this. But I was changed after this.

Experience.

Chapter 6

Entanglements

I am a body.
I have a body.
I am a body.

I roll these words around like marbles in my mouth as I sit in traffic, grateful for the air-conditioning system and half-listening to Bruce Springsteen. I am on my way to an appointment with my acupuncturist. I cannot yet not cringe internally at the fact that I now have an acupuncturist. The year 2020 changed me in all kinds of ways, but the way that it changed my relationship with my body was probably the most profound transformation.

I finally took my self, my body, seriously, as an entity worthy—in need—of care in 2020 after a series of, as Lemony Snicket would have it, unfortunate events. I was struggling at work at the end of 2019. A pointed comment about my performance at a particularly vulnerable time for me cascaded into meetings with management, the compilation of dossiers, and endless phone calls with union representatives and university HR. The 2019–2020 bushfires in Australia turned summer skies toxic orange, triggering anxiety that was immense, unfathomable, and unresolved by the meager coping strategies I had in place at that time. I had no way of balancing my deep need for respite with my inability to find rest. I was referred to an excellent therapist, and I worked harder. I tore my left calf muscle at martial arts training, which I began as a way of alleviating stress. The injury was extraordinarily painful, and disruptive. I was due to fly to London a few weeks later, to interview for my dream job. I traveled on crutches, and white-knuckled my way around the side streets and seminar rooms of Lincoln's Inn Fields while I was there. I had lunch with my mum in Covent Garden on the day after I arrived, and I had no idea that this would be the last time I saw her for many more months, as my world moved ponderously into stasis. I flew back to Sydney on March 12, 2020. Australia's international borders were closed eight days later.

I was exhausted when my husband and I made the decision to keep our child out of school, two weeks before the New South Wales government made that decision for us. My university provided "COVID leave" but this was, it transpired, not for use to mitigate the effects of the disease, but only for the disease itself:

> *If a staff member needs to stay home to provide care to someone as an indirect result of COVID-19 (example: school/day care closure, dependent asked to self-isolate) then the staff member should consider discussing work from home arrangements, if they cannot work from home, take carer's leave or if carers leave is exhausted, staff can apply for annual leave or other forms of paid or unpaid leave.*

And so we homeschooled, and I worked on. I was exhausted when we shifted teaching online and worked out how to use lecture capture, and break-out rooms, and Google hang-outs to foster the kind of community we had grown used to nurturing in physical spaces together. And still, we worked. I took on new students, submitted projects, organized reading groups, and wondered why I wasn't sleeping. I was exhausted when I learned the new vocabulary of pandemic disease, and learned how to navigate Zoom, and how to sit with my child as they cried, and I cried, and we grieved the loss of the year we had planned. I was exhausted, and I had no way of comprehending this. Eventually, my body found ways to make me understand.

> *I hope this finds you well. I am writing to you as my supervisor to provide a medical certificate to support my leave applications: one day per week for the next two weeks.*
>
> *With the additional challenges presented by homeschooling and working from home, I have been struggling to manage ongoing stress, and it is having a negative effect on my health. I saw my GP today, and he suggested in the first instance that I take a day per week sick leave for the*

next two weeks, and then evaluate my health after that. I have therefore
applied for this leave and attached the supporting medical certificate.

I cried helplessly in the office of my doctor, a slightly nonplussed
stand-in for my regular GP, as I recounted the migraines, the insomnia, the digestive issues, the recurrent chalazions that had driven me
into weekly appointments with an ophthalmologist and a twice-daily
routine of soaking and bathing my inflamed and reddened eyelids. I
tried to explain that it was all *too much*, that I was overwhelmed, and
sleepless, and unable to surmount each day, to *survive*. I took some time
off. I had a minor surgical procedure on my left eyelid, and the same
week I was put under general anesthetic for an endoscopic biopsy of
my stomach. I lay in the ward afterward and cried silent tears because
I had woken up from the anesthetic and I don't understand those tears
to this day. For a few months I worked a compressed week, and then
the university changed the policy that permitted flexible work arrange-
ments for academic staff. More migraine. More insomnia. More—and
worse—abdominal pain. And still, I worked. I spoke to my therapist; I
participated in life. I collapsed quietly, inside.

One of the friends who had commiserated with me and supported
me through all the tests and tears suggested that acupuncture might
offer at least a measure of relief. She offered this somewhat tentatively, recommending her acupuncturist to me as "a very sensible
human"; this friend knows me well. In January 2021, I cried again in
the acupuncturist's quiet and dimly lit office; again I tried to explain
that it was all *too much*. I had written "migraine, IBS, insomnia,
general decrepitude" on the intake form. I laughed, and cried some
more. She asked when I had last rested well, and still I cried, tears
of hopelessness and exhaustion and grief and desperation. She asked
how long I had been running on pure adrenaline, and I was utterly at
a loss, and terrified.

I was afraid that I wouldn't know how to do this job *without* running on pure adrenaline. Mine has been a career of the mind, with no
care at all for its fleshy support system. I have been both lucky and
good (and the former is still better), but most of all I have been willing to work *more*, work *harder*, work without concern for the ache
in my shoulder that twinges when I have spent too long in front of
the screen, work past the point of hunger or bodily need; my willingness to engage in this mild, socially acceptable, and professionally

rewarded form of self-harm is probably responsible for most of my success.

Previously, I had assumed that I was stressed because I was busy. Over the last few months, I have learned that I make myself busy because I am stressed. It was something of a revelation to realize that the same dynamics that powered my disordered eating for a decade and a half were now driving my "productivity" at work; with a shift in emphasis and a twist of external accountability, I have found new—less obvious, more self-contained—ways to convince myself that I am still falling short, ill-disciplined, imperfect, and new means of correction. And the academy applauds me for it. Whereas twenty years ago parents, doctors, and friends would urge caution, or plead with me, or otherwise try to mitigate (validate) the harm I was doing to myself, this new improved version of obsessive "self-improvement" is met with plaudits, promotions, and awards. And behind all of these achievements, there is less and less of me: less body; less heart; less care. I am unproduced in all this productivity. I have (been) dis-integrated.

Now I have acupuncture every couple of weeks. I practice yoga, and I meditate. I feel the vibration of my sankalpa even as I move around the world: *I am restored*; *I am nourished*; *I have healthy and energetic boundaries.* I hold on to these intentions. I have a way to go on this journey; I am still sleepless, and migrainous, and intolerant of most nightshades, soy, gluten, dairy, caffeine, refined sugar, and possibly onions. The prospect of a life without onions saddens me immensely. But I am only now beginning to hear my pain, the pain of my body, and recognize it as my own. I am only now beginning to learn that I am in need of integration, to learn how to descend into myself, and to feel on a cellular level the entanglement of my spirit and my substance.

I am a body.
I have a body.
I am a body.

I have said on many occasions that I cannot write my self out of my work, that my "I" voice is integral to the work I produce and therefore demands to be present. And yet I have tried to write my self out of my work daily—more specifically, tried to write out and write over and write despite my body, and its needs. In my mind I am always here, writing, as though the hands-arms-shoulders that connect my thoughts to the page are irrelevances at best, inconveniences at worst when they cramp, or chill, or err clumsily. Part of this is me, for sure, and whatever drives my obscene perfectionism, my need to produce and be perfect and be praised. But part of this is not me, or rather it is in the meeting place of me and the academy and the sticky suckering surface of our union, and it is in the institution's imperative to produce and be perfect and be praiseworthy. To sacrifice our selves to the higher cause, to the calling. Academia is a death cult. Pass it on.

* * *

A demon still lives behind my left eye. This is how I have come to think of my migraine, how I have learned to co-exist with the pain and disruption it brings. On a bad day, with a crippling sensitivity to light, nausea, and the feeling that the blood flowing to my brain has slowed to a crawl and is the poisoned consistency of pancake batter, I feel the presence of this demon keenly. At other times, it is a simple pressure, a pulsing awareness of its presence expanding into the space behind my eye socket, a familiar reminder that debilitating pain and brain fog and nausea might arrive at any time but, for now, this is a good day.

On the first day of the 2015 Project Q Symposium, the demon was in a tricksy mood, rather than out for blood: this was a vestibular migraine. The symptoms of this particular neurological condition are dizziness, loss of balance, and sensitivity to motion. When the demon manifests in this way, I feel constantly as though I am falling—falling over, falling out of place. At the Quarantine Station in Sydney, or Q Station, as it is known, where the Q Symposium was held, my pain and my present aligned: I felt out of place, I felt I was falling out of place.

I did not expect to like Q Station. It is the former quarantine station used by the colonial administration to isolate immigrants they suspected of carrying infectious diseases. Its location, on the North Head of Sydney and now within the Sydney Harbour National Park, was chosen for strategic reasons—it is secluded, easy to manage, a passageway point on the journey through to the inner harbor—but it has a much longer historical relationship with healing and disease. The North Head is a site of Aboriginal cultural significance; the space was used by the spiritual leaders of the Guringai people for healing and burial ceremonies prior to colonization and the removal of the Indigenous inhabitants.

So I did not expect to like it, as such an overt symbol of the ongoing violence of settler colonialism, but it disarmed me. I walked up from the ferry wharf and reveled in the views across the Head, the grassy richness of the slopes, and spaces between the low buildings reconditioned and reclaimed as accommodation and conference facilities. It is a place of great natural beauty and while it bakes in the fierce Australian sun there is a care about the space, a gentleness. We were welcomed to the country by, and invited to participate in, a smoking ceremony to protect us as we passed through the space, a reminder that this is not, was not, our place. That we were out of place. The entanglement of history and culture and land ritualized in the ceremony was a reminder also that I have not learned to reflect on the ways I am entangled with land, and culture, and history. I am caught in the in-between, careless, and headlong out of the now, away from the past. I am often out of place.

We were all out of place at the Q Symposium. That was the point. Organized by colleagues at the Centre for International Security Studies, Project Q, of which the Q Symposium is a part, aims to explore peace and security in a quantum age, in part through a series of symposia held at Q Station year by year. Positioning us thus was deliberate; we were to see whether voluntary quarantine would produce new interactions and new insights, to see how quantum theory "responds to global events like natural and unnatural disasters, regime change and diplomatic negotiations that phase-shift with media interventions from states to sub-states, local to global, public to private, organised to chaotic, virtual to real and back again, often in a single news cycle."[1] We sat, and we walked, and we talked, and we were tangled in webs of concepts across paradigms, out of place across disciplines.

I felt out of place. Mine was not, is not, the language of quantum theory. I learned much from listening to my fellow participants, but I was insecure; I was not only physically but intellectually feeling as though I was continually falling out of the moment, struggling to maintain the connections between what I was hearing and what I thought I knew.

Quantum theory departs from classical theory in the proposition of entanglement and the uncertainty principle (or more properly,

---

[1] You can learn more about the symposium on the Project Q website: https://projectqsydney .com/q-symposia/about-q2/.

apparently, "uncertainty relations"[2]), which states the impossibility of simultaneously specifying the precise position and momentum of any particle. In other words, physicists cannot measure the position of a particle, for example, without causing a disturbance in the velocity of that particle: "the more precisely the position (momentum) of a particle is given, the less precisely can one say what its momentum (position) is"—it is in fundamentally uncertain relation.[3] I do not know anything about quantum theory—I found it hard to follow even the beginner's guides provided by the eloquent speakers at the Symposium—but I know a lot about uncertainty. I also feel that I know something about entanglement, perhaps not as it is conceived of within quantum physics, but perhaps that is the point of events such as the Q Symposium: to encourage us to allow the unfamiliar to flow through and around us until the stream snags, to produce an idea or at least a moment of alternative cognition.

My moment was caused by fetal microchimerism. Scientists have shown that during gestation, fetal cells migrate into the body of the mother and can be found in the brain, spleen, liver, and elsewhere decades later.[4] It has even been suggested that microchimeric fetal cells are reparative, responding to maternal tissue injury.[5] This possibility delights me. There may be parts of my child in me: they may be healing me literally as well as simply metaphorically (the latter was already clear). "I grew you in my body," I say to my child—in awe, in love, in order to persuade them to take the bin out so I don't have to. I grew my child in my body, and there is a part of my child that is always in me. We are enmeshed, creatures of hyperempathetic connection. I have felt small strong fingers hold my face and stare intensely at the arrangement of my features, heard a small voice ask "But are you upset, mummy?

---

[2] Stanford Encyclopedia of Philosophy, "The Uncertainty Principle," 12 July 2016. Online, at https://plato.stanford.edu/entries/qt-uncertainty/.

[3] Stanford Encyclopedia of Philosophy, "The Uncertainty Principle."

[4] Keelin O'Donoghue, "Fetal Microchimerism and Maternal Health During and After Pregnancy," *Obstetric Medicine*, 2008, 1(2): 56–64; Amy M. Boddy, Angelo Fortunato, Melissa Wilson Sayres and Athena Aktipis, "Fetal Microchimerism and Maternal Health: A Review and Evolutionary Analysis of Cooperation and Conflict Beyond the Womb," *Bioessays*, 2015, 37(10): 1106–1118.

[5] O'Donoghue, "Fetal Microchimerism and Maternal Health During and After Pregnancy," p.57. See also: Olav Lapaire, Irène Hösli, Rosanna Zanetti-Daellenbach, Dorothy Huang, Carmen Jaeggi, Susanne Gatfield-Mergenthaler, Sinuhe Hahn and Wolfgang Holzgreve, "Impact of Fetal-Maternal Microchimerism on Women's Health: A Review," *Journal of Maternal Fetail Neonatal Medicine*, 2007, 20(1): 1–5.

What is your face saying?" because my child's heart feels the heaviness in my own. If they are restless, I am convinced that I can feel on a cellular level when they are soothed, when they give in to sleep. I can sense my child's disturbance if they are unsettled; their joy fills my heart. I am better for knowing and being with them. I am entangled with them in ways that I cannot comprehend.

I am not a scientist. I am a messy body always out of place, my self apparently composed of bodies out of place. My world is not reducible. My uncertainty is vast. All of these things make me insecure and challenge how I move through professional time and space as I navigate the academy. But when I return home from my time in quarantine and joyfully reconnect with my family, I am grounded by how I perceive my entanglement. It is love, not science, that makes me a better scholar.

Perhaps I am not proposing entanglement as Schrödinger does, as "*the* characteristic trait of quantum mechanics, the one that enforces its entire departure from classical lines of thought." Perhaps I am just using entanglement to denote the inextricable, inexplicable relationality that I have with my child, my family, my community, and humanity. It is this entanglement that undoes me, to use Judith Butler's most eloquent phrase, in the face of grief, violence, and injustice.[6] Perhaps this is the value of the quantum: to make connections that are not possible within the confines of classical thought.

But if this is the case, I must ask: why do we need a quantum turn to get us to a space within which we can admit entanglement, admit uncertainty, admit that we are out of place?[7] We are *never* (only) our "selves": we are always both wave and particle and all that is in-between, and it is

---

[6] Judith Butler, *Undoing Gender* (London: Routledge) 2004, p.19.

[7] In the time elapsed between my drafting these reflections and publishing this book, Laura Sjoberg wrote a very thoughtful essay called "Quantum Ambivalence," in which she discusses her reading of Laura Zanotti's book *Ontological Entanglements*, described as "in many ways the best of quantum IR." Sjoberg goes on to express her ambivalence about the book in terms with which I am intimately familiar, having witnessed and participated in several quantum discussions myself, and with which I sympathize completely: "Not very often does one come across an impressive and *desirable* book in IR. At the same time, despite my attraction to *Ontological Entanglements*, my ambivalence towards it remains. The very complexities that make it seductive are the ones that are both conceptually unnecessary (we can understand relationality, contingency, and uncertainty without quantum physics) and politically problematic (given the gendered and raced implications of reading science as authority, and the lack of clear and necessary political commitment)." This is, in essence, the source of both my discomfort and my irritation with quantum wonderings. Laura Sjoberg, "Quantum Ambivalence," *Millennium: Journal of International Studies*, 2020, 49(1): 126–139, p.136.

our being entangled that renders us human. We know this from philosophy, from art and the humanities—from love. So why can we not *learn* this from love? Why must we turn to science (again)?

* * *

I have attended many professional functions that I did not want to attend. I have held many glasses of cheap, warm wine and wondered, one eye on the exit, when I can reasonably escape home, or at least to the temporary comfort of my hotel room, to close the door against the day and exhale into my solitude. It can surprise people, apparently, to learn that I feel anxious and awkward at social events; their surprise does not surprise me, necessarily, because I learned to fake it well. I remember a line from a book I read years ago, which lodged in my throat: *children of divorced parents learn to hide their hearts.*[8] I have lived the truth of that, and it has stilled me, quieted me, and kept me in place when I wished to be elsewhere. It has, at times, kept me debating meaning, form, and content beyond my own boundary of boredom. It has compelled me to listen when I really want—need—not to hear, but to feel.

Listening only gets me so far. I have had to learn to listen to my body and to unlearn frozen, awkward, debilitating stillness, quietness, and stuckness in place. One of the things I learned early, in my first academic job, was to be still, to disavow my body, quell movement, and control both tone and volume of my speech in a bid to be perceived as *serious* in this academic setting. *Serious* people, I learned through observation, are still and quiet and emotionless in delivery. I noted this with the traces of an anthropologist's curiosity that clings to me still, and reflected: it is specifically white men who are still and quiet and emotionless in delivery. White men are serious people. I observed how patterns and displays of emotionality disciplined colleagues and marked out others as ill-disciplined. I played along, swallowed fear and outsider-feeling, and took my place among the still, white, men. I remain somewhat horrified at the ease with which I took on this form, and I wonder how different the environment might have been had

---

[8] This is, I am almost certain, from a book by Nick Hornby, but I don't remember which one and I don't remember the exact quote (or perhaps I do, and this is it). This is how I remember it, anyway.

I—had more of us—been bolder. What if we had been permitted what Arlie Hochschild calls an "unpatterned, unpredictable emotive life"?[9]

As Sara Ahmed notes, "'emotion' has been viewed as 'beneath' the faculties of thought and reason";[10] emotion is encoded with gendered and racialized power and rationality—emotion's tightly bound, tightly wound other—afforded authority in the value schema of Western institutions and their hierarchies, including within the academy.[11] And yet the currency of connection is emotion; being held in relation, belonging is *felt*. I can neither know, nor write, what I cannot feel. There is a duality here, an entanglement of feeling and knowing, and its expression, in writing.

While you and I have lips and voices which
are for kissing and to sing with
who cares if some oneeyed son of a bitch
invents an instrument to measure Spring with?

Each dream nascitur, is not made . . .[12]

To bear dreams, to bring dreams into the world, seems the province of lips and voices, of feeling and not abstraction and I wonder: how possible is it through writing in a register in which I was not trained, to conjure kissing and song with the same clumsy words with which I, *we*, claim—audacious though the claim may be—to measure Spring. Each dream, each dream *nascitur*: is born, begotten, *not made*. To begin to know how to bear dreams: that is to write. And yet we write this out of our selves, we train it out of our students; we repress, we deny. We demand a distance, a clinical reckoning, a disavowal, without accounting for the cost—without accounting for our selves. We are entangled in structures of meaning-making that demand we disappear.

---

[9] Arlie Russell Hochschild, "Emotion Work, Feeling Rules, and Social Structure," *American Journal of Sociology*, 1979, 85(3): 551–575, p.552. See also Arlie Russell Hochschild, *The Managed Heart: Commercialization of Human Feeling*, rev. edn. (Berkeley, CA: University of California Press) [1983] 2012.

[10] Sara Ahmed, *The Cultural Politics of Emotion* (London: Routledge) 2004, p.3.

[11] Ahmed, *The Cultural Politics of Emotion*; Nirmal Puwar, *Space Invaders: Race, Gender and Bodies Out of Place* (London: Bloomsbury Academic) 2004; Adia Harvey Wingfield, "Are Some Emotions Marked 'Whites Only'? Racialized Feeling Rules in Professional Workplaces," *Social Problems*, 2010, 57(2): 251–268.

[12] e. e. cummings, "voices to voices, lip to lip . . . (XXXIII)." Online, at https://www.americanpoems.com/poets/eecummings/voices-to-voiceslip-to-lip-xxxiii/.

If we tried to imagine (if we can) a language that avoids all ambiguities, multiplicity of meanings, and ill-defined words, and that insisted on near-perfect links between words and things in the world, this language would seem to be useful for talking only about the empirically most discrete realities. We might use it for talking about physics but not politics, electrons but not ethics, matter but not mind; a descriptive language that faithfully avoids the idols of the marketplace includes "brain" but not "soul," "useful" but not "virtuous," "oxytocin" but not "love."[13]

My professional self has developed and has grown in this environment; I am here but not here. I am unknowable and all-knowing: write with certainty, claim authority, and perform expertise. Bend words like softened bamboo, like reeds, be screened away. The whole of me is required and yet I cannot be whole here. I am, instead, eroded. There is nothing soft, generous, or nurturing, about the architecture of the building in which my office is housed. I try not to read this as a metaphor.

what is happening in those spaces of unknowability?
(maybe flowers)[14]

It is raining outside as I write this, and I am glad to have already gone for a walk today. I began walking daily as a form of meditation in 2020, before I learned other paths to more healthy stillness, and other ways to care for my self; as an exercise in mindful engagement with the environment that nurtures me, I took photographs of flowers. I have hundreds of photographs of flowers saved to my cloud storage and still on my phone. I thumb through them in idle moments, and they please me. They are a reminder that I am learning to look, and to look after myself.

At the end of 2020, I invited a dozen colleagues, mostly PhD students and post-doctoral researchers, to spend the day at Q Station. Like the earlier symposium, the idea was that we would convene in place and use the space to prompt reflection on the past year. I did not plan much, trusting that we would follow our feelings and make sense and make meaning of the event, and the preceding exhausting, demanding, disorientating twelve months, together, which we did. My concession

---

[13] Sam Matlack, "Quantum Poetics," *The New Atlantis*, Summer/Fall 2017. Online, at https://www.thenewatlantis.com/publications/quantum-poetics.

[14] I found this weird little fragment of text in the notes I took at the Q Symposium in 2015.

Flowers. Photos by author.

to planning was to order collages of my flower photographs, a copy for each person present, with a marker pen to inscribe an intention on the reverse to guide them through the coming year. Mine is pinned to the noticeboard in my office, showing flowers to the world and pledging to the soft felt wall: *Do less. Rest more.* I have not done so well with this intention. But the purpose of meeting at Q Station was to connect as a community, consider the challenges of the previous year, and figure out ways to survive and support each other in 2021. This, we did well. And part of our experience was the dis-location, our being out of place, as envisaged by the convenors of the Q Symposium several years before. Place matters. Land nurtures and soothes. Dreams are conjured in place; "Each dream *nascitur*" in place.

As I watch the horizon in between each tentative word-thought, I am reminded that the ocean is in me. Though I was born in South London, into rough gray concrete and Conservative party rule, into riots and the long terrifying shadow of nuclear war, it is the shoreline that soothes me and heals me whole. I am not home, and yet I am home when I am here. My heart is relaxed and expansive in these places. As fiercely as I feel a disconnection with the country I was born in, and the violence of its legacy and its present, the land is not the people and the land brings me peace; in ways that I do not quite understand, these places hold me up and let me stand. The gray coastline and downpours of the North Norfolk coast, the damp grassiness of Grantchester meadows, and the gritty sand trails through Thetford forest: these are the places I hold in my heart, that hold my heart steady.

I reside on stolen land currently, an impossibly insufficient term. To acknowledge land as stolen is too small a linguistic construct to hold the genocide of a people, the decimation of culture, and the diminution over many decades of ways of knowing, being, and doing. I knew next to nothing about the colonial history of Australia when I moved here in 2010, had been taught next to nothing about the brutal-ity of my country of birth and only its triumphs (though admittedly I dropped history as a subject in high school at age fourteen, so my historical knowledge more generally is sketchy at best). I have tried to learn, alongside my beautiful child, as the public school system here attempted an education in the horrors of colonization and it has hurt my heart. I have written indignant emails to indifferent teachers about the wild insensitivity of learning materials and it has hurt my heart. My pain remains, though, an alibi for racist violence,[15] and anyway my pain is not the point.

---

[15] Alison Phipps, "White Tears, White Rage: Victimhood and (As) Violence in Mainstream Feminism," *European Journal of Cultural Studies*, 2021, 24(1): 81–93.

My entanglement with this country is inflected always with not-belonging, with useless horror and flickering anger and quiet discomfort. To have found a home from home that soothes my soul but to know that my very presence here is an outrage causes dissonance that I compartmentalize and manage. I am still. I am here. I can be still, here; I am still here. I cannot begin to unpick the complex threads that hold me here, hold me in this place, even as I am dislocated. This shames me, even as I write. I am belonging, out of place.

Chapter 7

Epilogue

This is a book that was written across worlds. I feel so far removed now from the worlds that left their traces in the opening pages and throughout essays written earlier, in what I have come to think of as "before times." I can remember the circumstances of those opening sentences: how I had walked across campus in the late autumn chill, past the coffee stand crowded with people, into the building and freely up the stairs without the need of a swipe card or a face mask; how I had settled at my desk without morning ritual of cleansing invisible contaminants from my hands lest my commute pollute my keyboard and the unforgiving grubby whiteness of my desk, greeting colleagues in the then-much-used communal kitchen area or exchanging greetings in the corridors from a now-unsanctioned distance of a couple of feet; how I had written about privilege while knowing nothing of how it feels to spend eighteen months wondering idly when someone I love will die, wondering if I will ever see my mother again.

This is a book that was written in the fits and starts of a back-firing engine, because at times—much of the time—pandemic anxiety was a full-time job for me, and I struggled to make brain space for anything else. This book does not document the changes in my world since I began this (mis)adventure, but those changes are embedded in each reflection, woven tightly through the recounting of how I now encounter my surroundings. Those changes haunt me, and my writing, and each word seems so very small. I feel so very small. It is hard to feel significant in any way, in the

face of fire, floods, and pandemic disease. My anxiety spiraled beyond
my ability to contain or manage it after the bushfires of the 2019–2020
summer here in Australia, and I stopped writing for a long time. My words
didn't work in the way that I needed them to, not these words at least, in
which I tried to capture the fear and the helplessness and the hopelessness.
The words that would bring relief, or release, that would make me safe. In
the eerie swirling stench of that summer, I wrote only a little.

> *"Animal, vegetable, mineral . . .?"*
> *". . . Vegetable."*
> *"Is it bigger than a bread box (I mean, it depends on the size of the*
> *bread box . . .)?"*
> *"No . . ."*
> *"Is it a banana?"*
> *"No. Hang on. Just let me concentrate a minute, sweetheart . . ."*
> *I can't remember where my keys are. I know I can use my husband's*
> *car key to drive home if I have to, but I am filled with panic. I need to*
> *find my house keys. I scrabble in the pocket of my bag.*
> *"I can't find my fucking keys."*
> *I try to slow my breathing, try to think where I might have stashed them,*
> *as soft ash swirls around me. The doors are open but the car is loaded; the*
> *light is ochre and the fear is primal. I try to slow my breathing, and I remem-*
> *ber that I put the keys in a separate bag not ten minutes ago, a bag with my*
> *glasses and a water bottle and my phone, which I will want within reach*
> *when we are on the road. I suspect I will need to exchange the sunglasses*
> *I am wearing for the regular glasses before too long and I am not wrong.*
> *"Got them. Let's go."*
> *I aim for brisk but my voice is thin and edgy. Husband, child, and*
> *mother are quiet and efficient in their movements as they fold them-*
> *selves into the car. I briefly consider finding the property owner to*
> *notify them that we are leaving, but decide against it: we are already*
> *later leaving than I would like and the sky has darkened further in the*
> *ninety minutes since we made the decision to cut short our stay in the*
> *Snowy Mountains and race the fires back to Sydney. He will know that*
> *we have left when he finds us gone.*

Later, I tried, and failed, to explain the impact of the fires to friends and
family overseas when they inquired well-meaningly how I was coping. I
tried, and failed, to describe the horror that choked our coastline, charred

Journey Home, December 2019. Photo by author.

bush and parklands, destroyed habitats of humans and non-humans alike, to loved ones overseas who saw only apocalyptic media coverage showing walls of fire and images of children steering boats out to sea, away from the burning headland and the overcrowded beaches no longer providing safe harbor for people burnt out of their homes. I tried, and failed, to explain how this collective trauma triggered huge anxiety, how obsessively I refreshed news sites and social media for news of new fire lines and defense failures, how the residue of smoke in the air even now, some two years later, makes me edgy and restless. I tried, and failed, to explain to colleagues that no, it hadn't been a particularly restful or restorative summer. That I felt instead depleted, exhausted, diminished, and terribly afraid. I was not well, and I was not writing.

* * *

Once-in-a-century floods follow fire. Then, weeks after we fled the mountains under unbearable, unbreathable skies, the world shifted again, and we were suspended in a fractured restless time of profound uncertainty. I read lots of words, endless words, about how our perception of time changes when we are living through trauma, and again I write only a little.

On Monday, my day began at 7:00 a.m., giving feedback on a PhD student's research proposal and ended some fifteen hours later, when I gave up trying to contact a relative who is locked down alone and I finally managed to calm the insistent panic that they were not ok. They were ok, they just forgot that we had set up a call. Lost track of time.

On Monday, I learned about the three seasons of the Ancient Egyptian year and the key features of their agricultural production (Year 7 Human Society and Its Environment) and how to design a fair and reliable experiment (Year 7 Science). I reminded my kid to log in to Google classroom on the hour every hour and perform virtual attendance, because the school has been very clear that this is the only thing that they care about during these extraordinary times, and it takes less emotional energy to play by their rules than it does to point out all of the ways in which their rules surely don't apply at this time. To this time.

On Monday, I hosted the first weekly virtual coffee morning for colleagues in my department and listened to PhD students tell us about how hard it is juggling childcare, space to work, and in many cases completely redesigning their project because it's clear that the fieldwork they have planned for this year is likely no longer possible. I suggested that it was important to give these students space to grieve their lost projects, their other selves.

I held a meeting during which I pretended that I could imagine a day in the near future on which I would be able to sit down and put words together, and organize my thoughts and the thoughts of my collaborators, though it actually felt impossible at the time.

I listened to my husband supervise the afternoon's lessons and was brought to stillness by the recognition of how lucky we are, to have each other and my salary and secure—if rented—accommodation and high-speed internet.

I reviewed an article. I marinated chicken. I met friends for wine via Zoom and complained for an hour. I read—and wrote—emails about making up for a lost time, or rescheduling this or that event for a later time, and they hurt my heart because I can't imagine another time right now. I am crushed by the thought of the next hour. I cannot begin to imagine charting the territories of next week.

    At this time, I am always impossibly bridging a past (imperfect, beloved) life with futures unknown. I am full of feelings about the present moment. I am exhausted. I am grieving. I am enraged and frustrated and miserable and proud, and I have no way of managing or even beginning to comprehend the feelings that fill me. My therapist reminds me that I don't have to cope with my feelings, I can simply tolerate them until the urgency dissipates, and I can turn my attention outward again. But it is a lot, to ask a human to tolerate this feeling of fullness, when even the feeling of fullness fills me and I begin, just a little, to feel panic.

    I walk. I talk with friends. I watch trash television shows downloaded onto my iPad, listening to trite and clunky dialogue through the noise-canceling headphones that mark these forty minutes out as my time. I turn down the panic to a background hum: a hollowness in the stomach, a sigh, a clenching of the jaw, the quickness of my anger response when something confronts me. I catch myself, just in time. In time. Sometimes. But sometimes not. Some times.

    My reaction to social media posts about using this time productively is visceral. It tightens the back of my throat. I send a meme that says, "It's ok not to be at your most productive in a global fucking pandemic" to one of my WhatsApp groups. I am whistling in the dark. I write threads on Twitter and share articles about how these are not normal times. But I cannot suspend this time; I am suspended at this time, bridging.

    This time rips me apart. I am broken between the surety of times I have known and the terrible uncertainty of times to come. I am torn and contorted by this time and its pressure. I thought I knew time pressure, but this is the pressure of an unknown time. I stay with time, and I try to anchor myself here. But this time is not a time I can apprehend. My efforts to know it are fruitless; I try to grasp this time and my thoughts slide off and around its enormity. This time is glassy, impossible, and massive. I cannot find a way into this time, but I cannot cope with living across this time, I cannot suspend it. I cannot (can I?) sustain this bridging.

    And yet: I live across this time. I woke yesterday, and I will (I trust) wake tomorrow. I will eat, love, rage, cry, in time. I will sustain. I will

*be suspended. Perhaps this time is not to be used, or understood. Per-
haps this is not the time to rationalize or "manage" feelings. Perhaps
those are impulses borne of a different time. Perhaps within the expanding shell of this time, there is just chaos, and splinters of hope. Perhaps
I will feel my way to acceptance of disorder and be able to nurture the
pinpricks of contentment. In time.*

I have not yet found a way through time, to relate to and exist in time,
as the pandemic drags on and on and endlessly on. I don't know how
to *be*, in this pandemic-normal world. I wonder about how this time
will be judged, how *I* will be judged. I worry about the people I love
and bite at the skin on my lips until it bleeds. I follow the discussions
on social media about expectations, "under-performance," and lack. I
exchange messages with a dear friend who is exhausted from working
two full-time jobs, homeschooling her young children while "working
from home" to fulfill the responsibilities of her paid employment, with
no support, no recognition, no understanding, it seems, of the impossibility of splitting the self in this way. Not content with constructing
academics as infinitely fungible resources, the pandemic has demanded
of many this kind of splintering and in doing so caused desperation
and devastation. Hers is an ordinary, unexceptional, tragedy of time
and management, an object lesson on the elusive, illusionary *time
management*.

How should we manage time? How do we spend time? I find
increasingly that care takes time. If I am to do the things that keep me
balanced, help me sustain equilibrium, and stay grounded in times of
upheaval and fear, it takes hours out of my day, hours that I scrabble
for and steal back and spend walking, or breathing, or just staring at
the gum tree on the corner dancing in the wind. Exhortations to take
care mean little without a matching exhortation to take time. But even
in the new pandemic-normal, time is still not ours to spend. Rather,
time is to be used *productively*: learn a new language; bake (banana)
bread; teach yourself a new craft. Or publish, present, and plan new
projects—the industry will pay lip service to the distributed effects of
pandemic disruption, but I suspect those on hiring committees, promotion committees, and grant review panels will quickly forget that during this time of great leveling, when we were all in this together, some
were more in it than others.

Contemporary academia, at least the manifestations of it with which I am familiar—in Australia, the UK, North America—is, increasingly, a world in which we are required to measure our productivity, to account for "output" and "impact" along with dollars of grant income and numbers of publications, which are more easily quantified and thus stand as an estimation of value. As if the value can fit in the cell of a spreadsheet. Over the last two decades, academics in social science disciplines have learned how to measure all of these activities, to attach value to each, and we are the poorer for it. This is not an individualized problem, even as it is a problem that individualizes us; it is part of a broader shift toward "a quality assurance-driven audit culture"[1] within the academy, a recalibration of the structures within which we operate that now cohere identifiably as "the neoliberal university."[2]

While neoliberalism is a slippery concept for those of all political persuasions, its manifestation in the university setting revolves around "corporatisation, metrification, and performance-based funding models," motivated by the desire to secure a greater share of the global market in student enrolments than proximate competitors, based on "consumer preferences."[3] These processes are themselves driven by economic scarcity as much as (in tandem with) ideology, a result of the systematic defunding of public universities by successive governments in Australia and the UK and presumably elsewhere; "the market turn has transformed universities from being a cooperating set of public sector agencies, to being a hybrid and fragmented industry of contractors to the state."[4] Within the institutional walls of this industry—and within the walls of our own homes, and coffee shops, and libraries, as the contractors to the state now sub-contract labor in ways that render every academic interchangeable, vulnerable to market trends, and demand constant availability, intruding into previously "private" spaces (though this distinction was always tenuous for many) gradually and then all at once with the "work from home" directives issued at the onset of the covid-19 pandemic[5]—we are subjected to, and subjectified by, the will to measure.

---

[1] Briony Lipton and Elizabeth Mackinlay, *We Only Talk Feminist Here: Feminist Academics, Voice and Agency in the Neoliberal University* (Basingstoke: Palgrave) 2017, p.6.

[2] Lipton and Mackinlay, *We Only Talk Feminist Here, passim.*

[3] Lipton and Mackinlay, *We Only Talk Feminist Here,* p.6.

[4] Raewyn Connell, *The Good University: What Universities Actually Do and Why It's Time for Radical Change* (London: Zed) 2019, p.137.

[5] Margaret Thornton, "Coronavirus and the Colonisation of Private Life," *Legalities,* 2021, 1(1): 44–67, p.46.

The will to measure is exerted in hundreds of different ways throughout the career of every academic.

> [N]eoliberal apparatuses of the university work to construct our selves
> as lacking. We lack the qualities of a "good" teacher according to
> our student evaluations, we lack the qualities of a "good" researcher
> according to the metrics that quantify our inputs and outputs, we lack
> an Australian Research Council grant, we lack a publication in a "Tier
> 1" journal, we lack tenure, we lack a promotion, we lack the ability to
> cross the country for a conference, we are voids. There are huge gap-
> ing holes in our credibilities as academics, and we spend our days and
> nights, hours and hours, trying to plug up the holes, trying to stuff them
> with the cotton wool stuffing of appeasement, of reassurance, endlessly
> completing futile and empty tasks, searching for that moment of com-
> pleteness, of success.[6]

We are less than the sum of our parts, always, as we are reduced and
managed and made manageable by these technologies of administration; we are lessened by this bankrupt process of accounting. There is
rarely more of our selves to give, to account for, to express, and yet
we are never contained by the measures favored by our managers. Our
productivity, our performance, is assumed to translate with ease into
fields within annual planning and development forms, percentages of
student satisfaction, numbers of outputs, and citations to those outputs,
but how can they quantify the act of kindness that fosters community,
the expression of solidarity that reduces isolation and individualization,
the fulfillment of home-baked muffins brought to nourish colleagues
through another endless meeting?

I try to make different choices now. I have worked on visibility in
different ways, ways that are not always straightforward and are most
often quite terrifying, given—as touched on above—how precarious
the fiction that any of us are irreplaceable in the neoliberal university.
I have been an instrument, and I am flooded with the coppery taste of
shame when I recall my complicity with the fictions of measurements
that were wielded to discipline. I have benefited from this system, and
I have turned it against others. Perhaps there are shadows of atonement

---

[6] Eileen Honan, Linda Henderson, and Sarah Loch. "Producing Moments of Pleasure within
the Confines of an Academic Quantified Self," *Creative Approaches to Research*, 2015,
8(3): 44–62, p.47.

in my efforts now, in the acts that reveal my uncertainty, my vulnerability, at the same time as I know my white skin and my title afford me privilege that makes risks less risky for me than for others. And so, it is my turn to create and hold space for others, into which they can step forward; it is my obligation to use the privilege I have accrued to hold managers accountable, as best I can, for the damaging effects of their disavowal of shared humanity; it is my intention to listen and amplify those voices.

In the face of ongoing and relentless efforts to maximize our productivity and minimize our selves, putting effort instead into building circles of care is an act of radical resistance. Coming back again and again to the acts of kindness, the expressions of solidarity, the nourishment and nurturing that counter the numbness and the numbers ground me, and bring me joy. "There are moments, cracks and fissures, tiny spaces where we produce pleasure, when desire is released from the restricted codes of the academy"[7] and where instead of cells and fields and proclamations of peerless performance we find ways to connect, and be held, in relation. "Joy is a word not often spoken about today's market-oriented universities. But there should be joy in learning, in making knowledge, in solving problems, in sharing"; joy is in the connection, the community, the space between us that connects us and that we share.[8] "Spaces where we can 'talk feminist' are often spaces for repair, for healing wounds, for reflection and vulnerability,"[9] in which we remain alive to violence and exclusion and in which we nonetheless hold each other. We hold each other up, and to account, and in light. We work as though people matter. When asked what we have produced, we cannot—dare not—answer: our selves; each other; love. When asked how our productivity can be measured, we cannot—dare not—answer: it cannot.

Nevertheless, we connect, we support, we nurture and nourish; we stand together in solidarity and we survive. And I write, only a little.

Things I am no longer apologising for

I'm not ok
And I'm not sorry.

---

[7] Honan, Henderson, and Loch, "Producing Moments of Pleasure," p.52.
[8] Connell, *The Good University*, p.165.
[9] Lipton and Mackinlay, *We Only Talk Feminist Here*, p.104.

I'm not sorry that I don't have the energy today
To mask my inability
To focus on your words.
I'm not sorry that if you ask me how I am
And I let my body speak
And I say:
So tired,
And you sigh quietly
And say:
Anyway,
I will bite you
Or at least stare
Ferociously.
I'm not sorry that I haven't completed all the things
I imagined might be possible
And which can be counted
And make me count.
I'm not sorry
For celebrating with joy
Every tiny achievement
When some days sleeping and eating and tenderness
Are impossible.
I am sorry
That we shift uncomfortably
As I discover I need boundaries,
And learn how to articulate
That need even as I struggle not to
Fall apart completely.
And I am sorry
That I can't quite remember
The smell of my mother's skin
And the fullness of love
In her embrace.
I am sorry
About those things.
But those other things
I am no longer apologising for.

* * *

This is—a little, perhaps notionally, tangentially—a book about writing. Being, knowing, writing. Writing in academia, writing as an academic. Academia saved my life. It was December 2003, I was confused, conflicted, and clinically depressed. I was self-medicating, and I weighed no more than 110 pounds. I was a year into my PhD program. This was not my first go-around with depression and disordered eating, but it was the first time I had something outside of myself that I could lean on, invest in, and hope for. My supervisors called a meeting in which they expressed their support and suggested that I should suspend my enrolment, focus on my health. I cried, and shivered, and cried some more, grasping for the words that would help me explain what I knew: *I need this.* I didn't know then—nor do I know now—what *this* is, but it saved me, without question. Perhaps this is a story about how I try to save *this*, in return.

I have been unspeakably dreadful as a colleague, and a bad friend. A bad mother, sometimes, a bad feminist. I have said the wrong thing, backed the wrong decision, contributed to making the academy a less hospitable, less nurturing place. But this is not a story about my shame or my tears,[10] it is—perhaps, partially—a story about how even through all of the fumbling uncertainty about academic place and belonging and esteem and, amid all of the damage I have doubtless done, I am also learning how to be, and to know, in kind and generative ways.

The academy has shaped me, literally. It has put flesh on my bones, rounded my stomach, softened my angles, and smoothed off my sharp edges. I have grown a child in this body, which was unthinkable to me two decades ago. I have learned how to listen to my body, learned ways of coping other than to sublimate or suppress the exquisite glassy pain of self-doubt and hopelessness. I have learned to trust and to share, to let people go and to let people grow. I have supported people in their own ill-disciplined (ad)ventures and rejoiced in the insights and wordsmithing of colleagues, some of whom have become friends. Together,

---

10 As discussed in chapter 6, white women's tears can (be made to) function in all kinds of pernicious ways as an alibi for continued violence and oppression. Alison Phipps, "White Tears, White Rage: Victimhood and (As) Violence in Mainstream Feminism," *European Journal of Cultural Studies*, 2021, 24(1): 81–93.

a little at a time, we are changing the academy, and every one of their stories heals me.[11]

I have been tormented by the question of who this book is for. I suppose this book is for you, because here you are. But I suspect it is mostly for me. It is for all the stories I didn't tell, for all the times I bit my tongue and wrote my self out of my work. For all the times I turned away or folded my truth behind a polite smile. For all the fears and failures, and in all the restless dark hours, for all that I have felt that I am rootless, or never enough. For the grief, despair, uncertainty, the feelings that I never learned not to shy away from—that I learned instead to numb for fear they would engulf me, drown me, and end me. For all the being and knowing that I have yet to do.

I am learning to be present, to be generous, to love and let go, and to encounter with humility.

This is my self, and other stories.

---

[11] If you are looking for beautiful writing and/or world-changing insight about the academy, I recommend, among others: Naeem Inayatullah, ed, *Autobiographical International Relations: I, IR* (London: Routledge) 2010; Naeem Inayatullah and Elizabeth Dauphinee, eds, *Narrative Global Politics: Theory, History and the Personal in International Relations* (London: Routledge) 2013; Elizabeth Dauphinee, *The Politics of Exile* (London: Routledge) 2013; Maria do Mar Pereira, *Power, Knowledge and Feminist Scholarship: An Ethnography of Academia* (London: Routledge) 2017; Paulo Ravecca, *The Politics of Political Science: Re-Writing Latin American Experiences* (London: Routledge) 2019; Sara de Jong, Rosalba Icaza and Olivia U. Rutazibwa, *Decolonization and Feminisms in Global Teaching and Learning* (London: Routledge) 2019.

And So I Decided to Stay. Photo by author.

About the Author

Laura J. Shepherd is a professor at the University of Sydney, Australia. Much of her research focuses on the United Nations Security Council's Women, Peace and Security agenda, and attendant dynamics of gender, violence, and security governance. Laura is the author/editor of many books, including, most recently *Narrating the Women, Peace and Security Agenda: Logics of Global Governance* (2021) and *New Directions in Women, Peace and Security* (edited with Soumita Basu and Paul Kirby, 2020). She spends too much time on Twitter, where she tweets from @drljshepherd.

www.ingramcontent.com/pod-product-compliance
Lightning Source LLC
Chambersburg PA
CBHW031138270326
41929CB00011B/1680